Contents

THE FUNNY LITTLE MAN
The Biography of a Graphic Image

VIRGINIA SMITH

BARUCH COLLEGE
of The City University of New York

VNR VAN NOSTRAND REINHOLD
—————————— New York

Copyright © 1993 by Van Nostrand Reinhold

Library of Congress Catalog Card Number 93-3026
ISBN 0-442-01177-6

I(T)P   Van Nostrand Reinhold is an International Thomson Publishing company.
ITP logo is a trademark under license.

Printed in the United States of America

Van Nostrand Reinhold
115 Fifth Avenue
New York, NY 10003

International Thomson Publishing GmbH
Konigswinterer Str. 518
5300 Bonn 3
Germany

International Thomson Publishing
Berkshire House,168-173
High Holborn, London WC1V 7AA
England

International Thomson Publishing Asia
38 Kim Tian Rd., #0105
Kim Tian Plaza
Singapore 0316

Thomas Nelson Australia
102 Dodds Street
South Melbourne 3205
Victoria, Australia

International Thomson Publishing Japan
Kyowa Building, 3F
2-2-1 Hirakawacho
Chiyada-Ku, Tokyo 102
Japan

Nelson Canada
1120 Birchmount Road
Scarborough, Ontario
M1K 5G4, Canada

16 15 14 13 12 11 10 9 8 7 6 5 4 3 2 1

Library of Congress Cataloging in Publication Data

Smith, Virginia.
    The funny little man: the biography of a graphic image/ Virginia Smith.
        p.   cm.
    Includes bibliographical reference and index.
        ISBN 0-442-01177-6
        1. Commercial art—Europe—History—20th century. 2. Humor in advertising.
    I. Title.
NC998.6.E87S65   1993
741.6'7'09409041—dc20

                                                            93-3026
                                                            CIP

Preface and Acknowledgments

most designers have worked with French curves—those plastic templates that can be turned any which way to give you the arc you need, the line you want. History can be entered at any point, too, and an arc that we never noticed before can be followed, and for as long as one wants—it's not like a compass that makes a closed, perfect circle. The story of the FLM traces one new line in design history. This recurrent little figure puzzled and sometimes irritated me, and when I tested it on other graphic designers there was often the same reaction. I began to research its appearances on the pages of old German magazines. When I saw the FLM's connections with political figures, with persuasion and manipulation, with distortion, with the reception and rejection of images by different societies, I began to look at the image as an entry into understanding much more than design history. The book I wrote traces the arc cut by the FLM and describes its passage at significant points on that curve.

For permission to reproduce art work I am grateful to the following: the editors of *Novum Gebrauchsgraphik*, successor publication to *Gebrauchsgraphik* and *Das Plakat:* although it was not possible to locate all art from those publications, I appreciate the cooperation of the editors; the Artists Rights Society, as representative of ADAGP, SPADEM, and BILD-KUNST in the United

States, for Cassandre, Carlu, Hohlwein, Kandinsky, El Lissitsky and Leger; Thomas Rockwell for Norman Rockwell's painting *Breaking Home Ties;* International Business Machines Corporation, Bubbles, Inc., and Billy Scudder and Arlene Thornton Agency in Hollywood for IBM/Chaplin ads; Matt Groening and Fox Broadcasting Co., Inc., for the Simpsons; C. Raman Schlemmer and the Oskar Schlemmer Theater Estate; The Arrow Company, Inc., for J. C. Leyendecker; Paul Rand for his work; and the University Press of New England. I am personally grateful for: the wisdom of my editor Amanda Miller; the sensitive and witty art direction of Mike Suh; the insights and inspiration of graphic designers Henrietta Condak and Paul Rand; the suggestions of colleagues, especially art historians Christiane Joost-Gaugier, Eloise Quiñones-Keber, Amy Winter, and Gail Levin; the contributions of members of The American Printing History Association and The Society of Publications Designers; the translations of Karen Schlenker, Gertrud Kallinger, and Clare Galland; the valuable text suggestions of Sharon Lerner; the artwork of Satoka Funizaki; helpful information from Steve Heller, Eloise Lustig Cohen, Clive Phillpot, Charles Markis and Good Shepherd, Barbara Bruning McGhie; most important, the Library of Baruch College and its superior staff and librarians.

Introduction

biographies of human personalities can be intriguing; in one early chronicle the artist-writer Vasari documented the *Lives* of his Renaissance colleagues with enough dark hints (was Masaccio *really* poisoned?) to keep us interested. But there are limitations to biography, and especially in graphic design the events in a life may be less important than other forces acting upon the designer's work. Though we know that Alexey Brodovitch was a cavalry officer for the Czar, for example, only an imaginative editor could propose (as Diana Vreeland did) that the white areas of his pages recalled "the snows of his native Russia." Many biographies of artists and designers have been written. This book is a biography of a printed image.

The graphic image called the Funny Little Man (FLM) appeared in the early modern period, cropping up in significant centers of artistic activity. It was a representation of the figure in print, miniaturized and made humorous, designed for purposes of selling or persuading. Clusters of this image erupted in different places, designers spontaneously employing it to solve a design problem. Rather than a set of rules governing form, the variations of the FLM are linked only by similar impulses, creating the form in meaningful coincidences. From the First World War to the period of the cold war, hundreds of examples of the Funny Little Man appeared in periodicals and posters. He seemed part of the brisk confidence of early Modernism, and his disintegration coincided with its decline.

The FLM is a recognizable graphic type whose variations suggest some causes: the influence of fine arts movements, the effect of local political climates, the pull of traditional preferences. There is also the style of the individual artist (no small matter) and the possibility that the form itself can become exhausted. This exploration of the FLM suggests to the intended readers of this book—graphic designers and graphic design students—that their work has much greater implications than they realize as they sit before their drawing boards or computers.

As an image that appeared in posters, periodicals, and minor printed ephemera, the FLM is part of popular imagery. It is the creation of the graphic designer, a profession new in this century, still changing, but now establishing its history. Although there has been much attention paid to the history of graphic art, only recently has any been given to the history of graphic design. To most art historians, graphic art is taken to mean printmaking executed by a fine artist—woodcuts, lithographs, engravings—a separate body of work that draws its importance as a second medium of expression by a great artist—Goya, Kokoschka, Picasso. For graphic designers the work they do for reproduction is their main activity, and they do it knowing that it will be reproduced by someone else, a commercial printer, for a large, general public. They produce art with tools, colors, and imagination and they don't feel inferior to fine artists. In fact, most graphic designers would prefer to look at a beautiful poster by Cassandre than an oil painting by almost anyone else. Graphic designers are in a sense the descendants of early printmakers who produced woodcuts for broadsheets, printed for a public that scrutinized images of Martin Luther to determine whether he was a devil or a saint. That woodcut artist had great power to make the sixteenth-century public fear or admire Luther when they studied his portrait. Printmakers have been documented for centuries, both in histories of engravings, etching, and lithography, and in *catalogues raisonnés* of individual artists. Today graphic design is documented in histories of the alphabet, in studies of styles, and in biographies, all furnishing valuable material to the growing profession. This book presents another method, a narrative that follows an image carelessly invented, suprisingly revealing.

With hundreds of printed examples available, this could not be an all-inclusive survey of the FLM image. Many examples were omitted; those that were chosen had special qualities. In the narrative of the FLM, for example, Zietara is important not because he was a great artist but because his "moment of entrance," as Kubler puts it, was fortunate. Oskar Schlemmer was at a center of Modernism—the Bauhaus—during the period the FLMs proliferated; Schlemmer knew intimately the arguments and struggles of the early moderns, which he recorded in the letters and diaries he kept from 1910 to 1943. In the Soviet Union, Varvara Stepanova acted where Constructivism intersected with the FLM. Her importance as a theorist and designer is just now being acknowledged. Others were especially clear in their description of their creative processes—for example, there is the rationality of Carlu and Cassandre, or the special American vision of Rand. Most of these practiced both fine and applied art; most knew typography and design as well as painting and sculpture. And others are included because they provide the big, looming "other"; the opposite form that makes the FLM so noticeable.

The sources where the FLM can be found are publications and posters. He is truly a figment of modernism, a capricious product of imaginations flitting through an era distinguished by impermanence. All the places where he appeared were intended to be torn up, shredded, or burnt. A few fugitives appear here for a second viewing.

12. JAHRG.   JAN. 1921.   HEFT 1

DAS PLAKAT

→MÜNCHNER HEFT←

VERLAG DAS PLAKAT CHARLOTTENBURG

The Funny Little Man Arrives

Forms move and are born, and we are forever making new discoveries. KAZIMIR MALEVICH, 1915

the Funny Little Man first appeared at a time and place that ensured his successful future. This expressive little form, which we shall abbreviate to the FLM, was an early creation of the world of *"gebrauchsgraphik"*—German commercial art. In 1896 an art form had appeared in Germany that critics and collectors praised as a "new shoot" on the country's great artistic tradition. This development proved to be art for commerce—what the public named "commercial art" and designers today prefer to call "graphic design."

In 1896 a German artist successfully and consciously applied his original talent to publicity and launched the modern German poster. The artist, Otto Fischer (a young landscape painter), was neither imitative of such French poster artists as Jules Cheret and Henri de Toulouse-Lautrec, nor influenced by *Jugendstil* , the German version of French *"art nouveau."* Fischer's poster "The Old Town" won first prize in a poster competition for the city of Dresden and inaugurated a vigorous thirty-six year period of "utilitarian" art.[1] Posters and all forms of designed publicity, including advertisements, trademarks, and titles, comprised *gebrauchsgraphik*—art whose purpose was selling or persuading.

This early German commercial art flourished in two centers, Berlin and Munich. Artists knew Berlin as an intellectual center, but Munich remained "Kunststadt Munchen" (the art city), home

1-1 Valentin Zietara's cover for the Munich issue of Das Plakat, January 1921.

of both serious traditionalists and rebellious moderns. The Munich Secession rejected the painting of the art academies in 1892, and the Secession was in its turn displaced by Kandinsky's Expressionist group "The Blue Rider" in 1911. Over the first quarter of the twentieth century, Munich and Berlin developed distinctive poster styles: in Berlin a spare, flat look, in Munich a pictorial, humorous one.

In 1912 Valentin Zietara introduced the figure of a Funny Little Man, whose characteristics persisted for decades. Appropriately for a humorous figure, the FLM appeared in Munich, first in the work of Zietara, then by artists coveting his success. This odd new representation of the figure, with its diminutive size, simplified hands and feet, spherical head, and boneless body, appeared in Zietara's posters for tea, for a cafe (Figure 1-2), for chocolate (Figure 1-3), for tools, tubs and hot water (Figure 1-4). Zietara had hit upon a way of presenting mundane products with humor and appeal through the unpretentious little actor that he drew.

When the client manufactured a flexible product, such as yarn, Zietara formed his little man of those ropelike strands. If the client manufactured biscuits, the biscuits inspired Zietara to construct a person from pieces of zwieback, adding a round head.

1-2 *Poster for the Cafe Rathaus in Munich by Zietara, 1912.*

1-3 *Poster by Zietara, "My Bride Only Wants Zugspitz Chocolate," for a biscuit and chocolate factory.*

1-4 *Zietara's design in a poster competition for Krauss bathtubs.*

Much better trashy posters were being produced in the days when I had the pleasure of kicking in my cradle and there was no such thing as a science of advertising . . . .

Valentin Zietara, 1933.

The freedom Zietara enjoyed in forming an image of the human figure resulted in what today appear as strange, even bizarre, effects, but in his own time he was phenomenally successful, winning forty first prizes in forty competitions, and going on to win a total of seventy first prizes throughout his career. Although it was possible for Zietara to design in other styles, what was called his "peculiar way of delineating figures"[2] (Figure 1-6) became characteristic of Munich poster art.

Valentin Zietara had moved to Germany from his home in Poland as a young man, and he made Munich his home after studying design in Breslau. Zietara was a big, good-natured man, popular among his colleagues (Figure 1-5). He was cocky and irreverent, sardonic when mocking the theorists of the new "science" of advertising, but serious about his own practice. Zietara believed that the power of advertising resulted entirely from the talent of the individual artist, and he was skeptical of the theories of advertising put forth by new "propaganda" experts. Zietara was greatly in demand, quick and casual in his work, confident in his inherent talent to solve all his clients' needs quickly and successfully.

1-5 *Valentin Zietara.*

1-6 *Poster by Zietara, "Every decent man reads the Phosphor."*

By 1921 Zietara had refined his funny little man. It was simplified. It incorporated some of the abstractions of the fine arts. The corny, cartoon-like qualities were gone, and basic shapes of sphere and cylinder formed the head and body. In Zietara's poster of 1921 *(Bake with Yeast)* the mature FLM figure has become a vigorous abstraction (Plate C-1).

1-7 *Logo for "The Six" by Glass.*

1-8 *Design for "The Six" by Zietara.*

Zietara was the center of a group of Munich commercial artists who assumed the name *Die Sechs* (The Six) in 1914. Emil Preetorius, Max Schwarzer, Franz Glass, Carl Moos, Friedrich Heubner and Zietara were the six, although the membership varied. Glass designed the logo for the group (Figure 1-7) which Zietara incorporated into a design (Figure 1-8) and a poster (Plate C-2) announcing their connection with the Munich printing firm of G. Schuh. This arrangement ensured that clients who wanted designs by members of The Six had to have them printed by G. Schuh and Company. The coalition of The Six was only for business purposes; each had an independent style. Most prominent was Preetorius, an enigmatic theoretician and teacher, whose illustrations for the book *Peter Schlemihl* made his reputation.[3] Preetorius's drawing of the *schlemihl* figure used traditional proportions; his modernism appeared only in his use of flat colors, borrowed from the art that he admired—Japanese woodblocks. Another member of the group, Max Schwarzer, had the distinction of designing the cover of the publication *Das Plakat* for the 1914 issue, which featured Munich poster artists (Figure 1-9).

1-9 *Cover of Das Plakat in 1914 by "Six" artist Max Schwarzer.*

The burgeoning profession of art for commerce employed many *gebrauchsgraphikers* in Munich, and they replicated Zietara's FLM creation. Not only posters, but newspaper advertisements and promotional pieces for the artists themselves were accompanied by the diminutive figure. This unique and ubiquitous image, proliferating through the pages of the German mass

1-10 *A Funny Little Man by Julius Nitsche.*

1-11 *Two Funny Little Men by Gottleib Anders.*

1-12 *Two Funny Little Men by Hugo Frank advertising straw hats.*

1-13 *A Funny Little Man advertising "fine papers for all graphic purposes."*

media of the first quarter of the century, became an accepted icon of advertising. Hundreds of examples—by Nitsche, Anders, Frank, Nater and other graphic artists, from Stuttgart, Berlin, and cities other than Munich—establish this peculiar version of the figure as a phenomenon of the period. (Figures 1-10 through 1-13).

Graphic Designers at the Time of the First FLMs

Depicting the figure in the commercial art of the early twentieth century usually meant idealizing and glorifying it. In this tradition no one was more successful than Ludwig Hohlwein. A Munich illustrator, by 1925 Hohlwein was recognized with Zietara as an originator of the Munich poster, specifically the *Bildplakat,* or "pictorial" poster.

Hohlwein impressed contemporaries as a cultured, patrician genius (Figure 1-14). His grand studio on a residential Munich street was filled with golden lacquer Buddhas, gaudy stuffed birds, antlers—trophies from his hunts—and souvenirs from his foreign travels. When not riding or hunting with fellow sportsmen, he received them working at his drawing board in a cloud of English tobacco smoke; once a German prince rode into the studio on horseback. Considered to be Germany's premier draughtsman, Hohlwein's passion for nature had diverted him from the study of architecture to animal studies. His posters were an illustrated anatomy book of hounds, horses, leopards, and stallions—and majestic human animals as well.[4]

1-14 *Ludwig Hohlwein.*

Hohlwein's posters engaged the viewer by featuring a gloriously perfect figure, man or woman. Hohlwein drew the figure in athletic attitudes, swinging a golf club, or caught in solid, stationary poses (Figures 1-15 and 1-16) The limbs and features of these perfect people are correctly proportioned. If anything, their size is increased, the planes of their faces and bodies are sharpened, made more clear-cut. Hohlwein's treatment of anatomy, proportions, and pose all combine to form a "Great Big Man" very much the opposite of Zietara's "Funny Little Man."

Hohlwein, like Zietara, had imitators. Artists Karl Biebrach, Willy Wolff, and Lina von Schauroth imitated his nobly proportioned figures and his technique of covering the body with flat or patterned areas.

1-15 *Travel poster by Ludwig Hohlwein. © 1992 ARS, New York / ADAGP, Paris.*

1-16 *Poster for the Odeon Casino by Ludwig Hohlwein.© 1992 ARS, New York / ADAGP, Paris.*

In Berlin, on the other hand, the *Sachplakat* or "actual" poster developed. The *Sachplakat*, as it was then known, consisted of a bold illustration of the "actual" object or product being advertised—shoe, sparkplug, cigarette, typewriter, coffee beans—greatly enlarged and simplified, rendered in flat areas of color with contrasting highlights, against a flat, colored background. The brand name was in large, hand-drawn letters. This "actual" poster was the creation of Berliner Lucian Bernhard. Many copied his formula—Julius Gipkins and Hans Rudi Erdt became with Bernhard the chief practitioners of the "actual" poster.

Other prominent commercial artists—Deffke, Arpke, Baus, Klinger, Monkemeyer-Corty[5]—contributed to the poster's development. By the time the first World War broke out, the German poster, like the major Modern movements in fine art—Futurism, Cubism, Expressionism—had staked out its major stylistic territories, the "actual" and the "pictorial" poster, and the profession of *gebrauchsgraphiker* had been established.

The Influence of Frenzel

Early commercial art of the twentieth century, like other modern movements, rested on a theoretical basis. Editing *Gebrauchsgraphik*, a periodical that surveyed international advertising art, was the astute and passionate advocate of graphic design, H. K. Frenzel (Figure 1-17). Frenzel was commit-

1-17 Oskar Berger's caricature of H. K. Frenzel, far right, smoking cigarette with colleagues at the Congress of Advertising in 1929.

Advertisement is the great edu-cator of the public, for it is only by means of advertisement that the public is continually urged forward to wider horizons and encouraged to hygiene and cleanliness.

H.K. Frenzel,
Gebrauchsgraphik #2, 1929.

Little as I understand of the sci-ence and art of advertising—and it is both a science and an art—yet I honor and recognize its inherent purpose: to let the world share the advantages accruing from a facilitated exchange of goods . . . . if these efforts are crowned with suc-cess, they will have taken no small part in the solution of some of the most important eco-nomic and social problems with which the world today is con-fronted.

Prince of Wales,
Opening the World Congress of
Advertising in London, 1924.

ted to the promotion of advertising art. He believed that its poten-tial power was great. With an enthusiastic conviction of advertis-ing's beneficial effects, Frenzel exhorted artists to use their com-mercial talents toward the accomplishments of great goals. During his editorship, which ran from 1925 to 1937, Frenzel assiduously documented the production of the *gebrauchsgraphik-ers*. He analyzed, compared, and collected the output of most major commercial artists. He organized conferences and pub-lished works and words not only by German illustrators and designers but by other Europeans and Americans as well. Occasionally he published comprehensive retrospectives. He con-ducted surveys among nations, soliciting opinions on the state of the art. The publication *Gebrauchsgraphik,* under his editorship, became the showcase for commercial art of all kinds from all countries. Frenzel consciously sought to include graphic artists from smaller countries, such as Hungary, and he gave equal time to such large competitors as America.

During its initial phase, Frenzel expressed utopian hopes for commercial art like those claimed by fine artists: Sant' Elia for Futurism, Corbusier for architecture, Apollinaire for Cubism, Mondrian and van Doesburg for De Stijl. This "utilitarian art," said Frenzel, educated the public. This was the art that they saw daily. Frenzel claimed that advertising taught the public about the habits and customs of other nations—more, he claimed, than science. He saw advertising as the great mediator between peo-ples, the facilitator of world understanding, and, through that understanding, world peace. Toward this goal he sponsored world congresses on advertising in Berlin and Philadelphia, which were attended by executives and artists from around the world. Frenzel went so far as to assert that "a purely humanitari-an and happy world, living its life in a better way, could be cre-ated by means of advertising."[6] At one of his Congresses, mem-bers advanced a plan for an advertising campaign for peace, recommending that such universal propaganda be sponsored by the League of Nations. Such were the ambitions for early com-mercial art. Frenzel encouraged practicing artists to see their work in this idealistic context, and he sponsored the formation of organizations of peace through advertising in France, England, Belgium, Spain, Portugal, and Canada. His outlook was always international, and, until 1933, hopeful.

Frenzel believed that business produced an art reflecting the artistic and cultural life of its times better than any other art form. Here he echoed the French writer Apollinaire, whose poems and critical writings of 1912 praised Picasso and Braque for introducing letters from signs and other public printing into their paintings, because "in a modern city those elements played an artistic role."[7]

During the years that *gebrauchsgraphik* evolved, political life in Germany was turbulent. Before World War I, and again after it, German political parties—Socialist, Spartacist, Monarchist—engaged in murderous conflicts. Germany's defeat in WWI ended with nearly two million people dead and four million wounded. The humiliation of the Versailles Treaty, the imposition of financial reparations, loss of territory, and admission of war guilt further demoralized the German people. This anguish, exacerbated by mutinies and violence, hastened the founding of the Weimar Republic in 1918.

In the Weimar period intellectuals looked for new answers to old problems, as did artists. They were not always political, but they were radical in their receptivity to new theories, their willingness to try new approaches, and their indifference to tradition. The Psychoanalytic Institute in Berlin trained analysts in Freud's method; the Warburg Institute in Hamburg engendered new scholarship, and the Bauhaus in Weimar reinvented the curriculum for educating artists.[8]

The Place of the Bauhaus

The Bauhaus enterprise began in 1919, the first year of the Weimar Republic, and its closing in 1933 followed by only half a year the end of the Republic. In its passionate commitment to Modernism, its experimental practices, and its idealistic hopes, Bauhaus attitudes were typical of the Weimar spirit. Expressing the period's revolutionary spirit, an early Bauhaus manifesto described the school as a "center for all those who, committed to the future and defiant of established orders, wish to build the Cathedral of Socialism."[9]

The form masters of the Bauhaus in Weimar, and the *gebrauchsgraphikers* in Munich, though exact contemporaries who lived just two hundred miles apart (and who sometimes used the same printer) inhabited two different worlds. A completely different strain of graphic design emerged at the Bauhaus. Director Walter Gropius aimed to unite the fine arts and the handicrafts, accomplishing what he termed a "reunion" between creative artists and the industrial world. His radical new curriculum attracted acolytes from all over Germany and Austria: the first class in 1919 pledged to Gropius that he "would not have to fight

. . . you won't believe it, how from Munich, for instance, they look upon "free" little Weimar with jealousy and longing . . . . And it really will develop into something very wonderful: the Bauhaus.

letter from Lyonel Feininger to his wife Julia, June 30, 1919.

We want to create a clear, organic architecture, whose inner logic will be radiant and naked, unencumbered by lying facades and trickeries . . . .

Walter Gropius,
The Theory and Organization of the Bauhaus, 1923.

alone" and swore that his "views, aims, and efforts represent the fulfillment of the wishes of many."[10] The artist-teachers swooned, too, at the new Weimar paradise: painter Lyonel Feininger, the first faculty appointment, moved into his new studio, given by "Dear good Gropius . . . a room at the top story, about 45′ x 45′ and at the skylight a curtain like the giant mainsail of a full-rigged ship—and the view! . . . here I shall be able to work."[11] Gropius hoped to graduate journeyman artists who would meet professional craft union requirements as well as the high creative standards of the Bauhaus masters. He intended that in the laboratories of the Bauhaus new standards for industrial production would emerge.

Gropius's conversion had come during the War, when experiences in the trenches convinced him of his social responsibility as an architect to devise a better world. In this hope he shared with Frenzel and so many other Moderns the dream of a peaceful new world achieved through art. Gropius foresaw a "universal unity in which all opposing forces exist in a state of absolute balance."[12] The modern building, for Gropius, would unify all the arts, as the Gothic cathedral had unified all medieval life.

In the cathedral of architecture, however, Gropius left few pews for commercial art. Though Herbert Bayer and Josef Albers experimented with typography, and Moholy-Nagy designed Bauhaus books, the main purpose of printing and graphic design was to publicize Bauhaus plays, exhibits, and theories. Only fourteen Bauhaus books were printed out of the scores of titles planned.

Representations of the human figure in Bauhaus art were not likely to share any of the properties of the engaging FLM, nor did they. Bauhaus theory concentrated on nonrepresentational objects and the fundamental shapes of triangle, circle, and square. When the human being was represented, as in the Bauhaus logo (Figure 1-18), the head was abstracted into a series of planes and lines. Abstraction, not representation, interested the Bauhaus masters and students. Through the innovative curriculum they explored the nature of materials—stone, wood, metal, clay, glass, fiber—and their application. Human figures appeared to Gropius mostly as walking architecture,[13] as designed by Schlemmer for the Bauhaus theater.

Gebrauchsgraphikers and *Bauhauslers* were opposites. In Munich, there was common sense, in Weimar, intellect; in Munich, art for the mass media, at the Bauhaus, for the sophisticated elite. The utilitarian artists collaborated daily with business, while the Bauhaus pondered: how can art and business be rec-

1-18 *The signet for the Staatliche Bauhaus, designed by Oskar Schlemmer in 1922 and still used by the Bauhaus. © Oskar Schlemmer, familien Nachlass, Badenweiler. Photoarchiv. C Raman Schlemmer, Oggebbio, Italy.*

onciled? The Bauhaus explored, the practicing artists practiced, a contrast personified by the poetic Schlemmer and the prosaic Zietara.

Bauhaus elitism was evident to its more sensitive inmates. Dismayed when he first saw the new modern houses Gropius built for the Bauhaus Masters, Oskar Schlemmer suddenly had a "mental vision of the homeless poor standing and staring while the Lord Artists sunned themselves on the flat roofs of their villas."[14]

Yet the very different communities of Bauhaus and graphikers shared idealistic goals, stemming from their common experience of World War I. Gropius's belief that "there is a Universal unity" is not far from Frenzel's claim for world harmony through the underlying "oneness" of the commercial public. Both optimistically predicted, in the long term, the peaceful unity of the world. Both reached beyond regionalism; in Gropius's cosmopolitan evenings the inclusion of the Swiss Klee, the Dutch Oud, the Hungarian Bartok; in Frenzel's pages a dogged insistence of the internationalism of the "art and science" of advertising. There can be no question but that the range of experimentation with all art forms was much greater at the school. And there is also no question that the commercial artists did not anguish about their creations, except when invited to by Frenzel. Yet their sense of themselves as something more than paid talent is obvious. They intended, as much as the Bauhauslers did, that their art could transcend its mundane limits and contribute to the betterment of humanity.

These parallel courses of "low" and "serious" design flowed along with little connection. Later, in France, A. M. Cassandre and other poster artists acknowledged the influence of the Bauhaus, and so did Russian designers. But in Germany neither group knew the other. This isolation proved costly. Some *graphikers* believed as passionately in their art and in the cause of international peace and understanding as did the more cerebral and articulate Gropius and Mies van der Rohe, and perhaps they sacrificed more. Frenzel apparently killed himself in 1937, when it became apparent that barbarism, in the form of the Nazis, had triumphed over hope and harmony. Mies and Gropius, however, "Architects of Fortune,"[15] and Josef Albers emigrated to the United States, Mies to head the architectural school at Chicago, Gropius to lead Harvard's, Albers the Yale School of Art. Today, most graphic designers believe they are the artistic descendants of the Bauhaus, not the plain *graphikers* of Berlin and Munich.

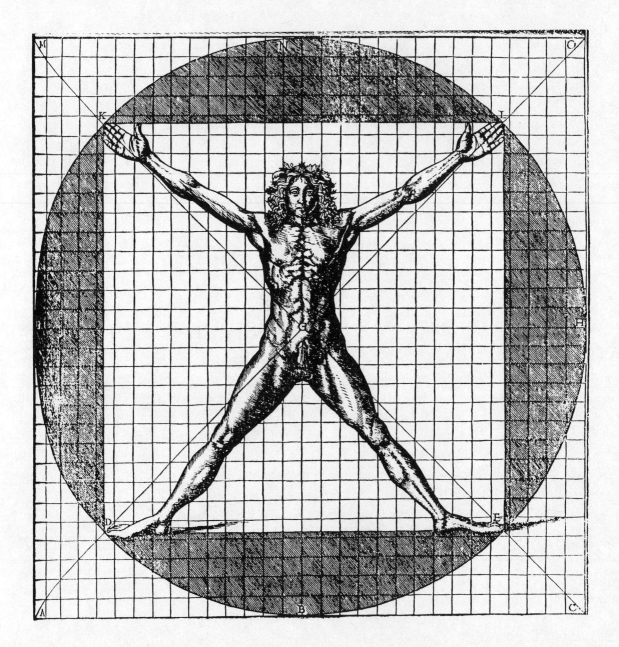

CHAPTER 2

Proportions of Meaning

*Representation of man will always form the great
metaphor for the artist*   OSKAR SCHLEMMER, DIARY, NOVEMBER, 1919

*The square of the ribcage. The
circle of the belly, the cylinder of
the neck, the cylinders of the
arms and lower thighs, the circles of the elbow joints, elbows,
knees, shoulders, knuckles . . .
the circles of the head, the eyes,
the triangle of the nose, the line
connecting the heart and the
brain, the line connecting the
sight with the object seen, the
ornament that forms between
the body and the outer world,
symbolizing the former's relationship to the latter. . .*

Diary of Oskar Schlemmer, written at the
front, October 1915.

2-1 *Measure of a man from the
1521 edition of* De Architectura *by
Vitruvius, written in 25 B.C.*

What impelled Oskar Schlemmer to analyse the representation of the figure so intensely was his view of humans
as cosmic beings. His version of the figure developed
at the same time as the FLM, but on a different track. By the time
he joined the Bauhaus at Weimar in 1921, Schlemmer had
already produced his revolutionary theater piece *Triadic Ballet*,
while a soldier in the German army. Almost as much an actor as
an artist, he performed in his own dances, and wore the abstract
costumes he himself designed. Gropius, first Director of the
Bauhaus and a practical architect and businessman, recognized
Schlemmer as an artistic genius (Figure 2-2). Schlemmer was sensitive and principled, and his amiable personality made him popular with Bauhaus students, whose relationships to other Masters
were often turbulent, their loyalties divided between Itten, who
dressed as a monk, and Klee, who rarely spoke.

Gropius asked Schlemmer to teach figure drawing, and with
that mandate he developed the course "Man." His notes for the
course show his awareness of historical methods of drawing the
figure, but he also recognized their limits. He alluded to geometry and the Golden Section and theories of proportion but
believed they were "dead and unproductive when... not experienced." He always wanted to discover and to be "surprised by
wonder."[1] Schlemmer conceived his course on man as both a
philosophical and an historical inquiry. Only such a passionate
conviction of the profound meaning inherent in the representation

2-2 *Oskar Schlemmer in 1932.*

The basic sense of proportion which every sensitive artist carries inside him . . . Klee instinctively uses very specific, biologically accurate measurements . . . the sense of proportion a man bears within him necessarily permeates everything he creates.

Diary of Oskar Schlemmer, May, 1922.

of the human figure could justify the persistence with which Schlemmer searched history for precedent and philosophy for interpretation.

In seeing man as "cosmic" Schlemmer meant that Man (always meaning male and female, the human being) was part of a universal order, and, as such, was connected to all other "references," or objects, in it. For him the human was both complete in itself and part of a much larger universe. As part of a larger universe of order, the creature "man" conformed to the principles of that order. Its underlying principles were what Schlemmer attempted to discover and to communicate to his students.

In the absence of a contemporary, universal, religious or political system to explain that larger order, Schlemmer sought answers in the natural sciences, in philosophy and psychology, in poetry and painting. Schlemmer's manifesto was "We the modern moderns!" His purpose was to persuade students to form their own views of the present after learning from the past.

Schlemmer's course was related to Bauhaus ideology in that it sought to design a better way of life. The study of proportions, he felt, provided insights that could be incorporated into other workshops at the school—furniture and housing, for example. It is easier to understand Schlemmer's concern with daily living, as shown in his notes on the "theory of hygiene, relationship with air, light, warmth, clothing, habitation, diseases and defence," when we realize that he himself was freezing in unheated lodgings shared with other Bauhaus masters, who wore fur coats indoors and laughed at each other's blue noses.

For Schlemmer, especially, the study of the body involved study of movement; he performed on stage and eventually directed at the Bauhaus theater—in fact, he held his figure-drawing classes in the theater. Instead of the familiar classroom with its dull and monotonous lighting, he relished the unconventional atmosphere created by spotlights, stage apparatus, and gramophone music. The sense of experimentation contributed to the willingness of students to pose nearly nude (for one hour). Schlemmer and the students analysed the results.

The Study of "Man" at the Bauhaus

Schlemmer's course on "Man" had three parts. The first section dealt with representing the figure graphically, the second with the scientific functioning of the body from birth to death. The function-

The head, to the tip of the chin, is divided lengthwise into four sections. The uppermost is the hair, the second the forehead, the third the nose, the fourth to the tip of the chin. This leaves the part below the chin . . . . Or else, take one eleventh part of the entire length; it will give you the face above the chin. The remaining portion is the hair above the forehead. Likewise, you will divide this eleventh of the length into three. It comprises forehead, nose, and chin. Behind the ear you also measure one third of an eighth of the body length. The ear is as long as the nose and half the width of the neck measured from the back to the bottom of the chin in a line with the beginning of the eyebrows and the point of the hair . . .

Albrecht Durer,
The Human Figure.

ing of the lungs, the heart as a pump, the sensual and sexual organs, the brain and nerves, were all in Schlemmer's "figure drawing" curriculum. The third part presented the thinking and feeling being, and ambitiously summarized the "basic systems of thought from antiquity until modern times." Here special modernist concerns with space and time, and, not least, the nature of the psyche—Freud had written all his major works by 1927—asserted itself. But repeatedly Schlemmer returned to the first segment, the drawn figure, to study theories of proportion, standard measurements, the Golden Section. He drew heavily on the notebooks of an earlier German artist, Albrecht Durer, whose interest in the figure equaled his own.[2]

Durer had studied the figure all his life, and Schlemmer copied from Durer's *Four Books on Human Proportion* and his *Dresden Sketchbooks* (Figure 2-3). Durer's analyses of the figure preceded his paintings and woodcuts, and satisfied his intellectual curiosity. An early Durer drawing of 1500 shows a nude "constructed"—that is, made of boxes, rectangles, and other geometric shapes—which Schlemmer imitated (Figure 2-20).

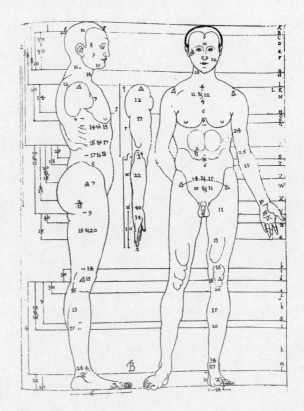

2-3 *Study of a nude man of eight headlengths by Albrecht Durer.*

*The handsome man must be
swarthy, and the woman fair.*

Cennino Cennini,
in Libro d'Arte.

Durer learned from a Venetian painter and printmaker named Jacopo de Barbari, who in 1500 had come to Nurnberg, where Durer lived, to work for the Emperor. Durer wrote, "I know of no one who has written about a system of human proportion, except a man, Jacobus, a native of Venice, and a charming painter. He showed me how to construct a man and a woman based on measurements. I was greatly fascinated by his skill and decided to master it. But Jacobus, I noticed, did not wish to give me a clear explanation. So I went ahead on my own and read Vitruvius."[3] Durer's constructed figures led him to extended analysis of the figure by measurement; that is, numbers and the numerical relationships of the parts to the whole. Usually the head was the unit of measurement to which all the other parts related.

Durer was not alone among Renaissance theoreticians in returning to Vitruvius, the Roman architect and author of *De Architectura*. When this work was discovered in the fifteenth century at the monastery of Monte Cassino, it became available as a source to Renaissance architects and other theoreticians of proportions. A new edition added 136 woodcut illustrations to the ancient text, causing the book to become a useful source for Renaissance artists.[4]

2-4 *Engraving by Pietro da Cortona in 1741, displaying the nerves of the throat.*

2-5 *Engraving by Pietro da Cortona in 1741, showing the muscles of the neck and the structure of the lungs, front and rear view.*

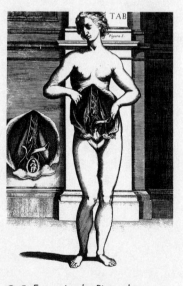

2-6 *Engraving by Pietro da Cortona in 1741, showing the female reproductive system, with an embryo.*

Many Renaissance artists were theorists, and their thoughts often started with Vitruvius. Durer, Leonardo da Vinci, Luca Pacioli, Pietro da Cortona, Paulo Lomazzo (Figures 2-4 through 2-6) and the French printer Geoffroy Tory adopted Vitruvius's notion of dividing the human body into ten parts. Vitruvius stated that the number ten could claim to be sacred because nature had given man ten fingers, and from them the palm of the hand was formed, and from the palm the foot. Ten was considered the perfect number. Any addition to ten invalidated it until another complete ten was added. Initially Durer drew a figure with ten, nine, or eight headlengths (Figure 2-7), but abandoned perfection to

2-7 *A striding man of more than eight headlengths by Albrecht Durer.*

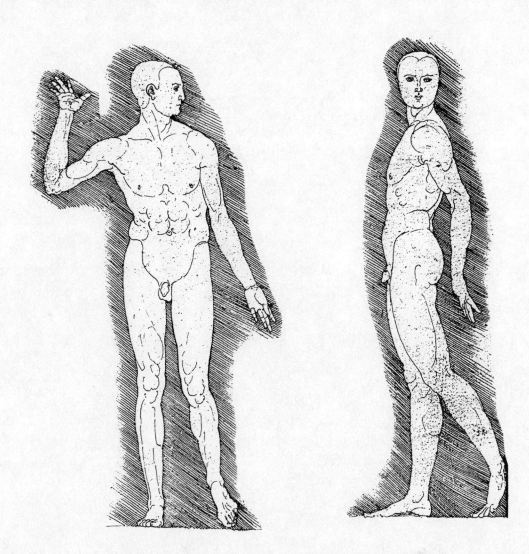

play with distortions of the figure—peasants and heroes, Tuscan chubbies, the old and the young, insane and deformed types (Figure 2-8).

Vitruvius believed proportion to be an adjustment of the size of different parts to each other and to the whole. This induced symmetry, necessary to buildings and to humans. He stated that nature had made the face, from the chin to the top of the forehead (or the roots of the hair), a tenth part of the height of the whole body. The forearm, the length of the foot, the width of the chest, all parts of the body were fractions of the height.

Both Schlemmer and Durer accepted this rule and made drawings of ten head heights. But Schlemmer abandoned it, as Durer had, to draw figures of other head lengths. Schlemmer's big figures showed his originality, which, like Durer's, became bored with perfection.

 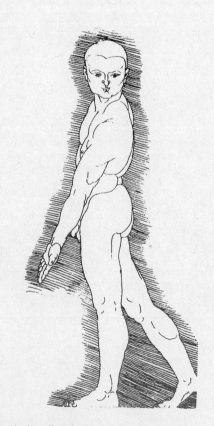

2-8 *A peasant man of seven headlengths by Albrecht Durer.*

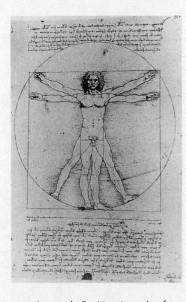

2-9 *Leonardo Da Vinci's study of human proportion, after Vitruvius (see figure 2-1).*

Scanning Renaissance canons uncovers other interpretations of Vitruvius. A familiar icon of proportion for graphic designers is Leonardo da Vinci's study of proportion with his notes. The figure of a man with arms and legs outstretched, standing in a circle (Figure 2-9) is on a sheet with da Vinci's quotations of Vitruvius's measurements, to which Leonardo added his own variations. Leonardo's interest in proportion, symmetry, and harmony led him to study the distortions from the ideal in the faces of the criminal and the insane. He attempted to plot their deformities through geometric analysis.

Leonardo's contemporary and friend, Luca Pacioli, focused his interest in proportion on what was "divine" about it.[5] Proportion, to Luca, was divine in the same way the deity was; as God could not be explained by words, neither could proportion be explained by numbers. Yet both these "hidden and remote" concepts—God and proportion—were unchanging and immanent throughout the universe, Luca thought.

To graphic designers, the knowledge that Renaissance typographers based their letters on human proportions is surprising. Studying Leonardo, and through him, Vitruvius, both Luca Pacioli

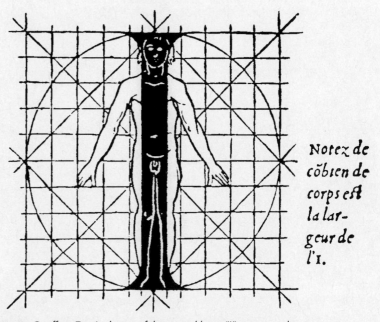

Notez de côbien de corps est la largeur de l'I.

2-10 *Geoffroy Tory's design of the capital letter "I" corresponding to an upright man, with ten sections, after Vitruvius, representing Apollo and the nine muses. Champfleury, Paris, 1529.*

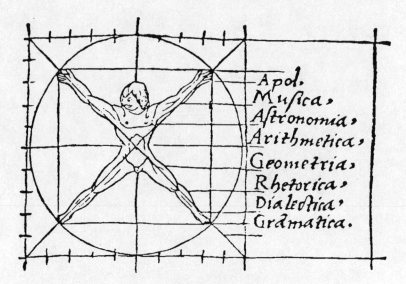

Apol.
Musica,
Astronomia,
Arithmetica,
Geometria,
Rhetorica,
Dialectica,
Gramatica.

2-11 *Geoffroy Tory's study of the letter from grid and an active man composed of eight parts, signifying Apollo and the seven lively arts: grammar, dialectic, rhetoric, geometry, arithmetic, astronomy, and music.*

and the Frenchman Geoffroy Tory constructed alphabets on a human figure.[6] Tory divided the upright figure into the ten Vitruvian sections (Figure 2-10). The capital letter was divided in the same way. With the rich and widely understood symbolism of the Renaissance at his disposal, Tory labeled the ten sections of the capital letter as "Apollo and the Nine Muses." He labeled the eight sections of a man with legs outstretched and shortened (Figure 2-11) as "Apollo and the Seven Arts"—music, astronomy arithmetic, geometry, rhetoric, dialectic, and grammar—practices that called for active participation, as the figure in action implied. The passive influence of the Muses he attributed to the stable, upright figure. With such colorful associations the Renaissance artist invested the figure and the alphabet.

In Northern Germany an amateur printer, the duke of Pfalz-Simmern, illustrated with his own woodcuts the publications he translated. These were studies of proportion drawn from the lively figures around his court—servants and nobility in the castle were his models. While acknowledging Durer's work, Duke Johann invested his own proportion studies with a graceful touch of the French and Italian renaissance, which he had imported to his own court (Figure 2-12).

2-12 *Woodcut by Duke John of Pfalz-Simmern showing his study of Durer's figures and perspective, 1531.*

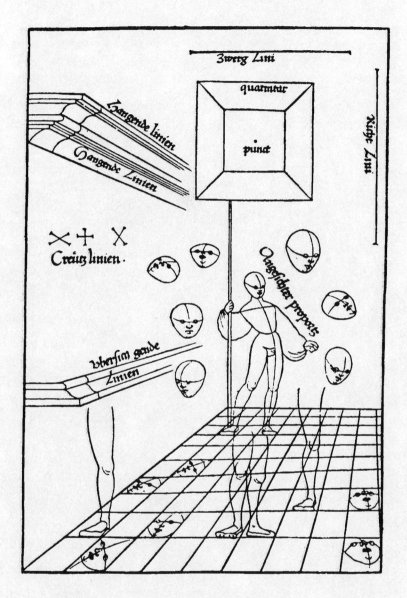

The body of Mars the god of warre . . . hath a long and slender body agreeable there unto; and may also serve for any other body of that nature; as being boysterous cholericke, cruel, martiall, mutinous, rash, and prone to anger; as are all active and strong men, by reason of the bignesse of their bones voide of much flesh, which causeth them to be of a harde and sharpe bodie, with great jointes, and bigge nostrels dilated with heate; whose eies, mouth and other passages are correspondent . . .

Paolo Lomazzo,
Tracte containing the artes of curious paintinge , 1590.

Paolo Lomazzo was a mannerist painter of Milan. When he was tragically blinded at the age of 29, he turned to theorizing about painting. Lomazzo, keeping the ten sections of Vitruvius, went further by attaching an appropriate temperament to proportions. The slender and comely body of a woman nine faces high, he wrote, was the way to depict Minerva, Diana—because of

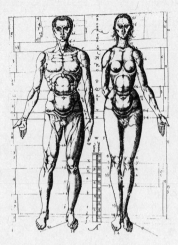

2-13 *Paolo Lomazzo studies of proportions of a man and woman, after Leonardo, Durer and Vitruvius.*

2-14 *Lomazzo's study of proportions of a horse, in his* Tracte containing the artes of curious paintinge *, 1590.*

her swiftness and agility—the Nymphs, the Rivers, and the Muses (Figure 2-13). In addition to proportion, Lomazzo's erudition allowed him to summarize the symbolic use of colors and gestures in the visual arts. Accepting animals as part of the ordered world, he analysed the proportions of their body parts. Lomazzo's tract of 1584 inspired the animal-loving English to publish it at Oxford in 1590, with tender studies of "the measures of an horse from limme to limme"[7] (Figure 2-14).

Studies of Proportion by the Ancients

Canons of proportion from Egypt of the third millennium B.C. establish the ancient human commitment to proportions of meaning. Priests were the only Egyptian caste with knowledge of the universe (however fanciful) and, since the carving of monumental sculptures was under their control, sculptural representations of the figure exemplify the priestly concept of the universe.

A singular aspect of Egyptian representations of the figure is that correct proportional representation of a dead person was necessary for that person in the afterlife. Most Egyptian sculpture was intended not for mortal eyes but to accompany the spirit of

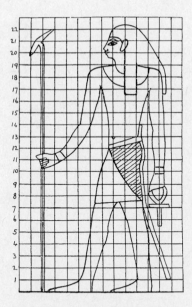

2-15 *The later Egyptian canon, from a tomb in the Egyptian Museum, Cairo, dividing the standing figure into twenty-two parts.*

The late canon.
Digital division of the cubit was . . . based on a tripartite division of the cubit into 1/3 cubit of 2 palms and its complementary fraction of 2/3 cubit of 4 palms, that is, the 2/3 measure . . . The principal units of this division were the thumb or inch, representing 1/12th of the 2/3 measure of 1 1/3 finger, and the fist. . .

Quoted in Iverson, Canon and Proportions in Egyptian Art, 1955.

the dead to the other world, where it would provide a body for eternity. So, the depiction of the deceased had to be exact. All parts had to be shown, for what was not shown was understood to be missing. In eternity the spirit would have no bodily form except this sculptural replica of its archetype—the person who had lived. And the dead person could not be shown in a momentary or fleeting action. His or her permanent, important defining characteristics, gender, and rank, had to be shown. Insignia of office, especially headgear, were included, to ensure the same rank in the afterlife. Going on the cosmic trip meant carrying your earthly status with you. Completeness was, in the literal sense of the word, vital.

Others—animals, servants, children, spouses—were represented on the same grid of squares as the buried person, because they existed in the same universe. But they were of lesser proportions. A wife, for example, might be the same height as her husband, because she shared his social rank, but she would be slimmer, and her hands would be smaller.

Features of the Egyptian Canon

Because so many examples of monumental Egyptian sculpture have survived, and because representation of the human body formed the principal subject matter of Egyptian sculpture, canonical proportions can be documented. Examination of Egyptian stone sculpture by early Egyptologists revealed lines drawn in red and black on the surface of the stone block from which the figure was to be carved. This implied the existence of a traditional canon of proportions. A professional sculptor must have known, looking at this grid of squares, where to place the main features of the body. Over time, two canons developed that account for most Egyptian sculpture. The earlier canon divided the standing figure into nineteen units; the later canon divides it into twenty-two units. The seated figure measured fifteen units in both canons. The later canon lasted until Egypt was conquered by the Romans (Figure 2-15).

The Egyptian canon standardized relationships of the parts of the body, starting with that of the thumb to the fingers, the fingers to the palm, the palm to the forearm, and the forearm to the height. The anonymous Egyptian craftsman could look at a stone block incised with a grid of lines, and place the knee according to the canon, on the 6th square, the elbow at the 12th square, the upper lip at the 17th.

Copying the round shape of the universe they [the gods] confined the two divine revolutions [the eyes] in a spherical body — the head, as we now call it— which is the divinest part of us . . . Accordingly, that the head might not roll upon the ground with its heights and hollows of all sorts . . . they gave it the body as a vehicle for ease of travel. And the gods, holding that the front is more honourable and fit to lead than the back, gave us movement for the most part in that direction. So man must needs have the front of the body distinguished and unlike the back; so first they set the face on the globe of the head on that side and fixed in it organs for all the forethought of the soul and appointed this, our natural front, to be the part having leadership.

Plato,
Timaeus.

Symmetry and Section in Greece

The Greeks knew the Egyptian canons. One Greek, Diodorus, recorded that it contained twenty two units. But the Greeks carved marble bodies not for the soul to inhabit in the afterlife but to immortalize Olympic winners and warriors, to honor gods and goddesses. Like the Egyptians, they aspired to correct replication of the human figure, but they used observation, not calculation. Concepts of proportion, symmetry, and *eurythmia* (grace) governed the making of their sculpture. Whatever their system, there is a quality of beauty in Greek sculpture that many viewers believe implies some geometric system for achieving beautiful proportions.

Archaic Greek workshops developed formulas that derived in part from the Egyptian canons. One fifth-century sculptor, Polykleitos, wrote a treatise in which he set out the principles of *symmetria*. *Symmetria*, to Polykleitos, consisted not of measurements, but of a philosophical consideration of "the perfect" or "the good" or "the beautiful" in proportions. Measurement implied meaning.

The Greek mathematician Euclid knew an ancient system of proportion called the Golden Section. In it the smaller part is to the larger as the larger part is to the whole (Figure 2-16). The Golden section[8] can be constructed with a compass. It can also be expressed by a series of numbers, called the Fibonacci series: as 3 is to 5, 5 is to 8, 8 is to 13, and so on, or written, 3:5, 5:8, 13:21. Early Renaissance printers sometimes designed pages of

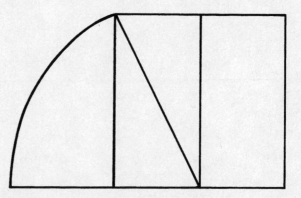

2-16 *Diagram of the Golden Section.*

Health is founded on symmetry, proportion or harmony of the elements water, fire, air and earth; however, beauty is founded . . . on the harmony of the parts, that is, in the relation of one finger to the other, of all fingers to the hand and to the wrist and of these parts to the forearm, the forearm to the entire arm and in general of all parts to all parts, as Polycletus demonstrates in his canon of right proportion or harmony.

Galen,
Greek physician, c. 150.

their books making the text area proportionate to the size of the page using Golden Section ratios.

A Medieval Sketchbook

An innocent and fanciful exploration on the shape of the human figure survives in a sketchbook made by a French architect associated with construction of great French cathedrals of the High Gothic period. This man, Villard de Honnecourt, may have worked for the Cistercian order of monks, or studied or worked on the design of Rheims, Chartres, Cambrai, and other astounding structures built between 1225 and 1250 in Northern France.[9] In his sketches he documents design elements in churches "now rising from the ground." Plans for the Chair for the Virgin Mary, the proper form for a crustacean, a cat, a bear, or a swan, as well as the City of Heaven, fill his pages. Towers and

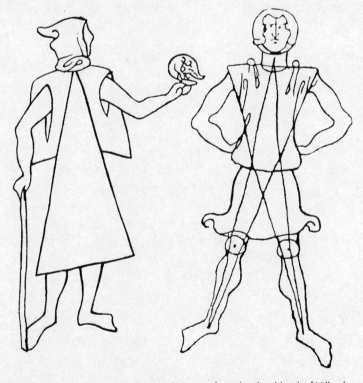

2-17 *A hooded falconer and a standing man from the sketchbook of Villard de Honnecourt. Manuscript 19093 of the French Collection in the Bibliotheque Nationale in Paris.*

Our holy proportion deter-
mines the formal appearance
of heaven . . .

Luca Pacoli,
Venice, 1509.

cups are equally important. Villard was as much interested in lion taming as in architecture, and delivered instructions on how both are accomplished. Villard sought the geometric forms underlying human and animal figures. He saw a " hooded faulconer" in a triangle, and a "mounted knight within an eight-pointed star" when observing his 13th-century contemporaries. He found pentagrams and five pointed stars in flowers, squares in a woman's face and hand, curves in "intersecting ostriches," and two triangles in a bearded face. His inscriptions on the pages indicate his intention to provide a "method of drawing as taught by the art of geometry, to facilitate working." His artist's eye discovered, through perceptive and careful observation, the forms that he lovingly and imaginatively presented (Figure 2-17).

The Modern Modulor

Fascination with the Golden Section has endured. It found a 20th century disciple in French architect Le Corbusier. In his obsessive study of measurements and the human figure, which he used to determine correct proportions for his buildings, Le Corbusier evolved a system which he called the Modulor.[10] Le Corbusier divided the figure into three sections (the Triad) or two (the

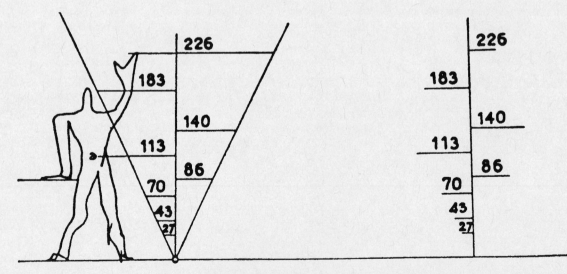

2-18 *The Modulor of Le Corbusier, based on the actions and proportions of a standing man.*

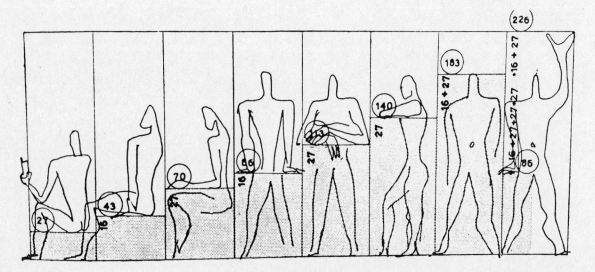

2-19 *The Modulor of Le Corbusier, showing the average man sitting, leaning, standing, and reaching.*

Duality) (Figure 2-18). He noted 113 centimeters as the center of the body, 183 as the top of the head, and 226 as the tip of the fingers of the upraised arm. He claimed that a man standing, with his left arm upraised and his right hand resting on a ledge or table top will touch the four points in space that a human figure occupies (Figure 2-19).

Le Corbusier tested the Modulor in the *Unité d'Habitation*, the utopian modern apartment building outside Marseilles. On the side of the building he placed a bas relief of the Modulor. As the heir to the Greeks, Le Corbusier carried an ancient system of proportion into Modernism and poured it in reinforced concrete.

Reviewing these efforts to arrive at a theory of proportion, it becomes apparent that most studies were made to determine what were *correct* proportions. The Funny Little Man we are following is an aberration, for it is deliberately rendered in *incorrect* proportions. Early artists studied proportion under the impression that its rules were there to be discovered. Moderns invented new rules.

The proportion trail from the Egyptians to the Greeks, through Vitruvius's texts to the new men of the Renaissance, into the Bauhaus with Schlemmer, and outside it with Le Corbusier, documents Schlemmer's claim that representation of the human

Should I say something about my beloved daughter? She inspires much admiration, is called "lovely young Greek" and "Mantegna child." I myself feel she has excellent proportions.

Oskar Schlemmer,
letter to Otto Meyer, March, 1922.

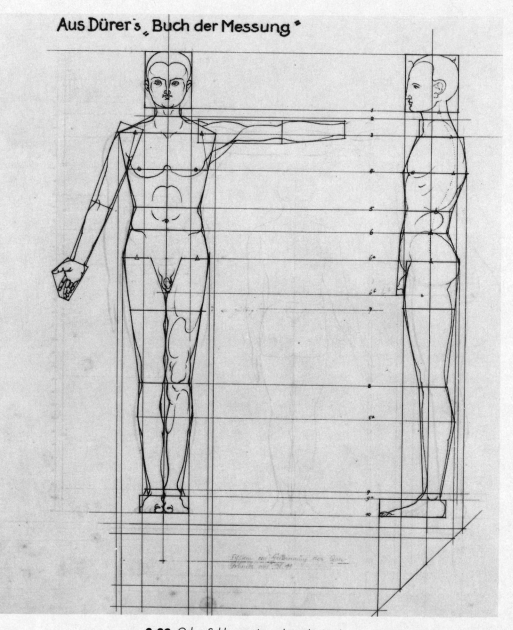

2-20 Oskar Schlemmer's study at the Bauhaus of Durer's "constructed" figure. © Familien-Nachlass OSKAR SCHLEMMER, The OSKAR SCHLEMMER Family estate, Badenweiler, Germany.

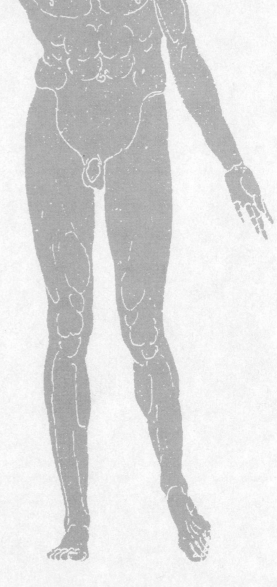

When modern mathematically minded artists examine the paintings of the Old Masters for classic proportions (the Golden Section, the Pythagorean formula) and find them present to a striking degree, this still does not prove that the Old Masters painted according to mathematical principles. There are many such startling examples of sure instinct, guided perhaps by the proportions of the human body, the hand, the characteristics of the joints. The eternal values may be found in the human, the divine. And thus in their depiction . . . This is the key to everything.

Diary of Oskar Schlemmer, May, 1922.

figure is the great metaphor. When he put his research into practice, teaching his course on "Man" at the Bauhaus, he found, by the end of May, 1928, both joy and sorrow. Sorrow, because the students were apathetic ("typical Bauhaus laziness")[11] and joy, because he himself was fascinated by "digging into" philosophy, anatomy and psychology before drawing the figure. To Schlemmer, as to all artists, it has always seemed that a deeper understanding of the world is somehow concealed in the flesh, and in the arrangement of its gangling parts.

CHAPTER 3

The Funny Little Man and His Friends

Open up at last your head
Leave it free for the demands of our age
Down with art
Down with bourgeois intellectualism
Art is dead

DADA SLOGANS, BERLIN, 1919

Why does the Funny Little Man differ so drastically from the representations of the human figure that we have just examined? This little icon was only possible in early modernism. The experimental movements in modern fine art gave commercial artists permission to make distorted forms. In a historical sense the FLM is distinctively an early 20th-century creation, resulting from its economic system and functioning in its devastated, fragmented, and fluctuating society. In earlier worlds human beings and all other animals existed in a universe under some governing rule, and such theorists of proportion as Dürer or de Honnecourt searched for evidence of ruling principles to apply to the human body. When art was deeply connected to rite or religion, to cathedrals and saints, man and woman, as creations of God, conformed to that order. Constructions of artisans conformed to the order of the universe—their beauty manifested its harmony, and their hands imitated the great creation of the heavens, moon, and stars.

Moderns were alienated from this past. Historically minded artists like Schlemmer realized what this loss meant to art. He noted the difference between artists of the past and those of his own time, trying to explain what he called the "bewildering array of artistic trends, and the desperate search for standards."[1] He concluded that the artist of the past acted as a "medium,"

3-1 *Four entries in a competition for Fix and Nochlich, all using Funny Little Men, 1919.*

expressing the values or religion of the people through artwork. He admired that richness: "What a wealth of individual artworks was inspired by the common ideal of Christianity! African sculpture and Greek statuary grew out of the culture of entire peoples . . . . But nowadays! Dilution, discarding, and destruction of old ideas."[2] Part of Modernism was to reject the past, but Schlemmer was one modern who blamed this rejection for the dour state of the modern artist, whom he saw as withdrawn and alienated. Modern artists conformed to no single religious belief, shared no common ideal. No common belief existed for art to reflect. Leaving the construction of the human figure up to each individual artist—Zietara, Schlemmer—was without precedent.

Artistic imagination had displaced a religious belief system. Since the 18th century, the Renaissance notion of harmonious, mathematical beauty had been questioned and replaced by what became known as creative urge, or the "creative will."[3] This impulse was independent, and perhaps superior, to metaphysical rules. Painters of the Romantic school cherished this belief, and their freedom became incorporated into artistic thinking.[4] After the First World War, this doctrine, combined with competition, allowed the creation of legions of original drawings of the figure in art, including early commercial art.

Description of the Funny Little Man

If there were only one employer of the FLM form, it would be no more than an aberration from the norm, just Zietara's quirky way of drawing. But the attributes of the FLM appear in Julius Nitsche, Ferdy Horrmeyer, Hugo Frank, Karl Fodsch, Walter Nehmer, Willibald Krain, and dozens of others, all of whom drew variations on Zietara's model. These multiply and reinforce the essential nature of the FLM. What do the funny little men populating the pages of these early German magazines have in common?

Zietara's early Munich posters for such breweries and bars as the Cafe Rathaus (see Figure 1-2), or the Pschorr Brau (Figure 3-2) featured a combination baby–man. These jolly, jaunty figures are not dwarfs and yet not proper adults. They present their products, related to alcohol, with smiles and gesturing limbs. In his Munich poster of 1914 for *Die Sechs* (Plate C-2), Zietara's figure is a jaunty boy. His malt coffee poster of 1913 used the baby–man (Figure 3-3), and a near–dwarf advertised "growth" bread for a baker. Even an aged man in the Tuto tool poster of

3-2 *Zietara's FLM for the beer Pschorr-Brau.*

1913 shrank to a mini–man. These early Zietara creations of the FLM were continually featured in *Gebrauchsgraphik,* where contemporaries praised them as novel, vital, effective advertising—absolutely the best representative example of the Munich poster.

Zietara refined his little figure in the 1920s. In the *Bake with Yeast* poster of 1921 (see Plate C-1) the little man evolved into a cubist arrangement of circles, cylinders, and rectangles, striding on an arc. In the later poster *Kunstler Plakate* (Figure 3-4), the FLM shed his dwarflike traits, and is artfully composed of smooth arcs and cylinders, his face an abstraction of curves. He is a modern abstraction of the finlike Zugspitz chocolate man (see Figure 1-3), also in tuxedo.

3-3 *An early Zietara poster for Kathreiners Malt Coffee.*

3-4 *Zietara's poster for Poster Art.*

These animated FLMs proliferated in ads for Munich services, stores and products. Nitsche's drifting form in *Das Plakat* of January 1921 is typical (Figure 3-5). Ferdy Horrmeyer dancers with anatomically impossible hands and feet appeared in a 1920 shop sign (Figure 3-6). One of the strangest FLMs is in a poster for the Berlin Reading Circle (Figure 3-7). An anonymous Dresden artist made a typical FLM for a 1925 poster (Figure 3-8). This flying figure with boneless limbs and contorted head is

3-6 *Ferdy Horrmeyer's sign for a shop selling signs, pictures, books, and games, 1920.*

3-5 *Nitsche's business notice in a 1921 issue of Das Plakat, the journal for friends of the poster in advertising.*

3-7 *The sponsor's poster for the Berlin Reading Circle, by Klusmeyer.*

less real than the trumpet he blows or the bell he rings. Another flying figure of Munich was drawn by Thomas Theodor Heine, the well-known *Simplicissimus* artist, for a book cover in 1918 (Plate C-3).

3-9 *Zietara's poster for punch, wines and liquor.*

Their Common Traits

What so many of these figures share is the act of balancing, tumbling, drifting, flying , slipping—a sense of instability. If balancing, it is precarious; if standing, it is temporary. Often they are, like Heine's man, sliding dangerously.

Their most obvious characteristic is, of course, their size. They are diminutive. Their bodies are small and their heads are large and round, and the impression they frequently give is of a cheerful child. The combination of the large, undeveloped head with the chubby, unformed limbs is a shorthand description of an infant (Figure 3-9).

Often their bodies are distorted beyond recognition. Their hands and feet are not functional; they could not stand or kick or march, or strike out. Their anatomical incorrectness makes it apparent that they only grab, they cannot grasp. This, too, is characteristic of infants. The FLMs are buoyant, ebullient, joyful. They have a sense of fun. Untroubled, they are not weighed down by anything, so they float and fly, tumble and dance, bounce around. Their chubby rubbery forms can be shaped many ways.

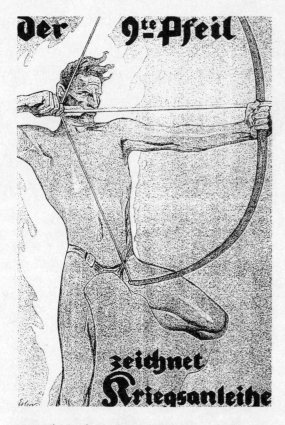

3-10 *"The Ninth Arrow Supports War Loans," a poster by Esler for a youth organization.*

3-11 *Poster by Meyer-Lucas, "Knock down the gates of peace and sign the eighth war loan."*

Together these characteristics connote a figure that is amiable, nonthreatening, helpless, happy, sunshine-spreading. A child. Perhaps a pet. Intuitively the Munich artists had found a form appropriate and acceptable to use to promote a product. This ingratiating figure acted as the product, and all its appealing and innocent attributes became the product's. There could be nothing dangerous about cigars, or beer, if this little fellow sold them! They were not even permanent, just a fleeting, appealing notion.

This interpretation is strengthened by looking at posters done at the same time and the same place, not for commercial but for patriotic purposes. In the Esler poster of Munich in 1919 *(The Ninth Arrow Supports the War Loans)* (Figure 3-10) and in Mayer-Lukas (Figure 3-11), the correct, well-proportioned figure fills the poster. The muscular hands firmly grasp their objects, the muscular legs are not about to fall. The solemnity of their purpose, related to war, intuitively evokes from the poster artist ideal proportion and true anatomy. The association of concepts like patriotism with stable figures and naturalistic or even enhanced proportions recurs later, more ominously, in the Nazi period.

So the FLM evolved as the pictorial representation of a commodity. He is a figure flying from the cigar factory and the brewery, into the vision of the urban stroller, whose library was the sidewalk, with its posters to be quickly skimmed, and its newsstands to be hastily scanned.

Hohlwein's Heroic Angle

The "other" Munich poster continued. By 1925 Ludwig Hohlwein, who was still based there, shone as a famous commercial artist, the "greatest master of the German poster" according to some.[5] Hohlwein's posters featured his own distinctive version of the human figure. Contemporaries insisted that the highest peak of artistic mastery lay in his portrayal of the figure. Hohlwein's big-boned athletes and musicians filled the area of the poster sheet, modeled on friends from the hunting and shooting world, princes, aristocrats and clubmen. Hohlwein's female figures were modeled on his "charming wife and daughters." These Grand Teutons embody Hohlwein's conviction that it was the artist's responsibility to preserve the German cultural civilization against the "onslaughts from the East," a contemporary code word for Bolsheviks in the new Soviet state to Germany's east.

This eruption of the Teutonic ideal contrasts forcibly with not only what reviewers termed Hohlwein's "droll little Chinese and Nigger boys" but with the hordes of flying and tumbling FLMs. Hohlwein's figures are not only large, they are statuesque, and, like statues, they are seen from a low viewpoint. The viewer looks up to Hohlwein's figures as a pedestrian looks up to a statue on a pedestal. This viewpoint requires what could be called a "heroic angle" of vision. Hohlwein's figures acquire their aristocratic, aloof quality from being beheld from below, and from being lit from below, which accentuates their strong jaws, aquiline noses, and deep-socketed eyes (Plate C-4). They are most often standing solidly; when seated they are relaxed, immobile. Their stability and solidity is everywhere enhanced—by frontality, by squareness, by frozen postures. They rarely move. When they do move, they are caught in a moment of balanced grace (Figures 1-15 and 1-16). Anatomically they are complete—all fingers and bones and muscles are included and emphasized. Intuitively,

We can reach our aim only when arts, crafts, and industries interpenetrate each other. Today they are widely separated . . . the crafts and also the industries need a fresh influx of artistic creativity in order to enliven the forms which have gone stale and to reshape them . . . .

Walter Gropius,
address to local crafts and industries
leaders, Weimar, 1919.

. . . these days the Bauhaus resembles a mad-house—there is flaring or brooding rebellion all around. Reason: the prize awarding . . . . What the students resented most was that Gropius had declared he would always intercede for the most extreme in art, as a manifestation of the times we live in.

Lyonel Feininger,
letter to his wife, June 27, 1919.

I am aware of the danger that lurks in the merely decorative, the degradation of high art to commercial art.

Diary of Oskar Schlemmer, November, 1922

Hohlwein, a self-taught artist, had placed the heroic figure at the heroic angle, implying the superiority of his characters.

How different they are from the flitting, tumbling mini-men of the FLM contingent! Every quality of the FLM—smallness, humor, distortion, instability, fragmentation, movement, friendliness—finds its opposite in the Hohlwein figure—giantism, seriousness, anatomical correctness, balance, completeness, stability, reserve.

It could be said that the Hohlwein poster was more of the *"graphik"* or artistic, side of *gebrauchsgraphik*, while the FLM occupied the more humble *"Gebrauch,"* or useful, half. Hohlwein's admirers scorned the "industrial magnates" and "merchants" of the commercial world and adored Hohlwein's aristocratic sportsmen with their binoculars and rifles, their fallen stags and hunting hounds. The FLM bounced along merchandising beer and taverns and milk, chocolate, and hot water for the home—a lower class of client.

But the FLM, common as he is, could not have developed without the experiments in form on a serious level that had been made by the revolutionary modern artists early in the 20th century. Before the outbreak of the First World War, the major modern movements in the fine arts of painting and sculpture had flung down their manifestos and exhibited their art. Modern painters and sculptors—whether Cubist, Futurist, Expressionist, Dadaist—used form as expression. They manipulated or played with form to make it do what they wanted, not to supply a naturalistic representation of the real world. Rejecting academic traditions and conventional draughtmanship and color, they distorted form for effect and for compositional purposes. Adopted by commercial artists, the fine arts techniques of exaggeration, abstraction, and simplification found their way into the mass media.

At the Bauhaus

While commerce and art were united in the *gebrauchsgraphikers,* though along the two different tracks of Zietara style and Hohlwein style, the Bauhaus, which in 1925 had moved to Dessau, constituted a third example of alliances between commerce and art. Stylistic shifts, ideological refinements, faculty rivalries, and student strikes kept Gropius occupied with internal matters. From its beginnings, the Bauhaus hoped to affect the popular world. Sales of its workshop articles were small at first, and mostly to an avant-garde clientele—Montessori schools,

3-12 *Oskar Schlemmer as the Turk in his Triadic Ballet, 1922. Copyright Bildarchiv Raman Schlemmer. Oggebbio, Italy.*

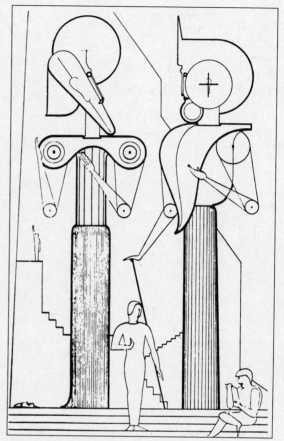

3-13 *Two monumental figures for the stage as high as the proscenium, designed by Oskar Schlemmer. They may represent Power and Courage or Truth and Beauty. Their arms are hinged, their voices magnified, and they move on wagons. The smaller figures have normal human dimensions and sounds. © Theaternachlass Oskar Schlemmer, Badenweiler. Photoarchiv C. Raman Schlemmer, Oggebbio, Italy.*

painters, architects. But with the Bauhaus exhibitions of 1923 its work became more widely known, and after moving to Dessau in 1925 and the establishment of a Bauhaus corporation, sales of pottery, textiles, lighting, and furniture increased. The first industrial contract was signed in 1928, but not until 1932 did the Bauhaus claim substantial revenues from commerce.

Throughout the years of changing curriculum, internal divisions, and local political opposition, Bauhaus Masters persevered in their serious explorations of art. Albers took over the color course when Itten departed, taking his vegetarian menus with him. Gunta Stolzl of the weaving workshop became the first female Bauhaus Master. Klee painted. Kandinsky devised an entire system based on his dogma about color and geometric shapes—the circle was blue, the square red, the triangle yellow. He reasoned that the circle was cosmic, absorbent, feminine,

3-14 *Schlemmer's figures transferred to the human shape, resulting in "ambulant architecture" depicting motion, rotation, and direction. It metamorphoses into a star from the hand, the infinity sign from the folded arms, a cross from the shoulders and spine.*

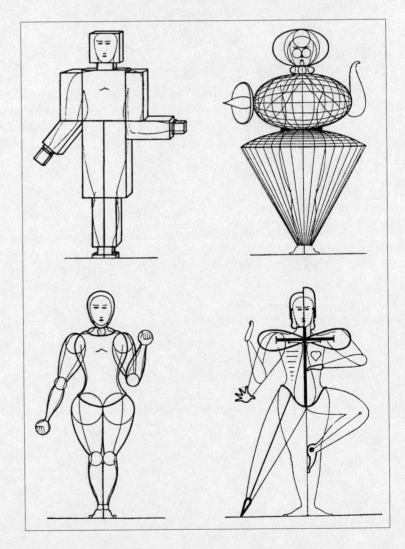

soft; the square active and masculine; the triangle a point. Every curved line he considered part of a circle, therefore blue, every straight line red, every point yellow, with infinite variations.[6] Most important, the Bauhaus had a new stage, and Oskar Schlemmer began systematically to create an experimental theater devoted primarily to study of types of figures.[7] His highly original conclusions were embodied in costumes for the *Triadic Ballet* (Figure 3-12), for his *Figural Cabinet* and the *Pantomime of Places,* as well as in imaginative drawings for proposed ballets.

Schlemmer associated size with lofty concepts. Monstrous pairs symbolizing "Power and Courage," "Truth and Beauty," "Law and Freedom" reached to the top of the stage, sometimes forty-eight feet high. Their mechanical voices were amplified by megaphones to match the grand scale of the figures (Figure 3-13). These giants were carried by wagons onto the stage where they contrasted with natural man, an actor with a normal voice.

Schlemmer discovered metaphysical meaning in his research on the forms of the human body.[8] He conceived four types of the human body: the cubical, composed of spatial–cubical constructions, resulting in "walking architecture"; the functional, where the body's movement suggested shapes of egg, vase, club, and ball in the limbs and joints; the moving body, with aspects of direction, rotation, and intersection, resulting in spirals, cones, and disks; and the metaphysical, where signs in the body—star, cross, infinity—implied meanings beyond the confining material of flesh. The extended hand formed the star shape, the folded arms on the chest the infinity symbol (Figure 3-14).

What came first, Schlemmer asked, with his customary triune divisions of thought—word, deed, or form? His metaphysical vision of the figure accorded with his wish to understand greater issues. (His analysis of theater began with the origin of life and the cosmos.) At the Bauhaus, colleagues like Wassily Kandinsky shared his mystical bent—Kandinsky authored *On the Spiritual in Art* for the series of Bauhaus books. Theoretical and intellectual, most of the masters searched for the fundamental laws of order in art, hoping to discover the equivalent of harmony in music, a hope never fulfilled. In the airy, glass-walled Bauhaus building at Dessau, students and masters pursued their ideal when not relaxing at parties disguised in silver masks and fantasy costumes. On snowy nights, passersby on the dark Dessau streets could look up to see Bauhaus buildings illuminated by metallic lanterns that cast shadows of dancing students and masters on the vast glass walls.

3-15 *George Grosz's sketch of types on the German street after the First World War.*

In the month of January they did weare white, in February ash-color; In March tawny: In April darke greene: In May light greene: In Iune carnation: In Iuly red: In August yeallow: in September blew: in October violet: In November purple: and in December blacke.

Paolo Lomazzo,
"Of Certain Other Colours" in Artes of Curious Paintinge, 1590.

Political Journals

In the real world, there was yet another style of figural representation. Caricatures in popular periodicals ridiculed the powerful and pompous. Two magazines, *Kladderadatsch* in Berlin and *Simplicissimus* in Munich, published German satire to an appreciative public. *Kladderadatsch* ,[9] the earlier of the two, had been founded in the revolutionary period of 1848, when the German Emperor relaxed censorship, allowing suppressed anger and criticism to erupt in the press. The magazine published satirical articles accompanied by drawings. It jeered at military figures like Bismarck, and introduced fictional characters like the reactionaries Strudelwitz and Prudelwitz.

Simplicissimus, begun in 1896, was politically liberal and composed mostly of drawings, with little text. It took its name from a 17th century novel in which the naive hero, Simplicissimus, roamed Germany noting its foibles and customs. Like its namesake, the journal *Der Simpl*, as it became known, encountered society.[10] But its look was far from naive. Such cartoonists as Thomas Theodor Heine, Edward Thony, Bruno Paul, and Olaf Gulbranson were fierce in their portrayal of hypocrisy, stupidity, cupidity, materialism, and every other vice. By the 1920s, the "corrosive bitterness" of the Simplicissimus artists was legendary.[11]

Both magazines paid a price for their boldness—prison sentences for the editors of *Kladderadatsch,* and lawsuits for the *Simpl* staff. But the brutal satire they employed risked it. The grotesque, distorted figures they drew had a moral purpose, as satire must, ridiculing wickedness to expose and correct it. And by directing its criticism against the powerful, they amused the public. The slashing lines and dark forms, the strong feelings, the antisentimentality of many of these satirical caricatures derived from Expressionism: some *Simplicissimus* artists, like George Grosz, exhibited in both galleries and magazines (Figure 3-15). A kind of "Pop-Expressionism" conveyed the message to the public, not with funny little men, but with bitter little guys.

Replacing Symbols

Oskar Schlemmer once perceptively remarked (and Gropius agreed) that it was "the mark of Cain in our culture that we have no symbols any more and—worse—that we are unable to create

Of Blew

*Azure blew, besides other signi-
fications that it hath, noteth
loftinesse of the minde, faith and
zeale, as the Franciscans say. It
was used by the Virgine Mary
in her attire untill the passion of
her sonne. Besides, many of the
Apostles used it. And Christ
himself is painted with a garment of this colour. And so the
Papists represent God the
Father, because Azure resem-
bleth the colour of the skie near-
er than any other. And Isis the
Ancient goddesse of the
Aegyptians had her Priests
cloathed in this color . . . And
Cicero used sometimes to weare
this colour, giving men therby
to understand that he bare an
aspiring minde. We read in
Hester that King Assuerus had
al his chambers hanged with
Blew, to shew the loftines of his
minde. And last of al we read
that the first priests of the
Hebrews did weare long gownes
with large sleeves of the Iacinthe
colour, upon which they put
their upper garment called an
Ephod in Hebrew, embroidered
with purple and set with the
Iacinthe and the Saphire stones,
which signifie devotion.*

Paolo Lomazzo,
"Of Blew" in Artes of Curious Paintinge,
1590.

them."[12] Without symbols, twentieth century figures had to be expressive with their very bodies. What had been lost with the loss of a common ideal, a pervasive belief system, and a universal religion were its pictorial signs. Modern "streamlining" had also streamlined or stripped the visual world of hundreds of indicators of meaning. Those symbols, attributes, colors, and emblems, the multitude of imagery once read in pictures, were no longer understood. What twentieth century city-dweller recog-

AUDACIA.

*Adspice quid valeant, quo tendant ardor amorque,
Curtius in terram se mittit magnus apertam.*

3-16 *The personification of
"Audacity" from Cesar Ripa's
Iconologia of 1758.*

3-17 *"Vice" is a depraved dwarf, out of all proportion, wrestling with a seven-headed hydra. From Ripa's Iconologia of 1758.*

VITIUM.

*Non parcit Patri, laceratum, quis furor ingens,
vecta terit curvis Tullia saeva rotis.*

Depravity

The personification of Depravity is a wicked-looking dwarf, all out of proportion, and with a squint. He has a dark complexion and red hair. Since everything about the dwarf—his size, his squint, and his coloring—are departures from the "norm" of human appearance, they are like vices, which are departures from the normal life which strives for virtue. Thus they are against nature, too . . . red hair, a squint, or a dark skin . . . indications of a vicious nature . . . . The whole image of Depravity or Vice is based . . . on the old idea that a pure soul expresses itself in good looks and fine proportions, and the opposite does the contrary.

Cesare Ripa,
Iconologia, Hertel edition, 1758.

nizes that the wolf is the slyest of animals, or that the cabbage symbolizes contentment with one's lot in life? That laurel, ivy, and myrtle are the plants of Apollo, Bacchus, and Venus? That Venus *is* Venus? Is it commonly known that a baboon recalls Thoth, the Egyptian inventor of arts and letters? The serpent and the hen, the palm and the oak, the lightning bolt, the pedestal and the arrow personified abstract qualities in visual form. Every culture had symbols, derived from fables, drama, history and allegory— Aesop's fables in sixth century Greece, Plutarch's *Lives* in Rome, Egyptian myth, Christian lore, African legend. The contemporary artist lamented by Schlemmer worked without the props of moral and mythic ideologies.

But remnants of visual meaning remain, though heavily disguised, perhaps because they are so deep in human nature. Hohlwein's figures have the solid, vertical solemnity of a column, and, indeed, in the Baroque emblem books of the eighteenth century, the column was a symbol of stability. The boldness of those who attacked the law or institutions was personified in a determined woman trying to topple the column (Figure 3-16). The quality of Decorum was represented by a young man calmly standing, straight as the building behind him, and Magnificence was on a pedestal before a columned portico. The personification of Vice (Figure 3-17) was short, active, and deformed. In emblem books such as Ripa's *Iconologia*,[13] these visual signs were read like words.

Some original though long-forgotten meaning hovered around such forms. And the perpetual symbol of innocence and playfulness, whether shown as putto, infant, or cherub, appeared in emblem books and paintings and architecture—in fact, in all art. The funny little men of Zietara and his colleagues, with their childlike aspect, send a signal of innocence. By instinct and not by imitation, early commercial artists had found all the proper visual qualities to convey, through form, an engaging, ingratiating, eager-to-please newcomer for the public—the graphic salesman.

CHAPTER 4

The Funny Little Man Gets Around

The seven marvels of the modern world are:
1. *the internal combustion motor*
2. *the S. K. F. ball bearing*
3. *the cut of a great tailor*
4. *Satie's music ...*
5. *money*
6. *the bare neck of a woman who has just had her hair bobbed*
7. *advertising*

POET BLAISE CENDRARS, PARIS, FEBRUARY 26, 1927

Advertising is the flower of contemporary life; it is an affirmation of optimism and pleasure; it distracts the eye and the mind. It is the warmest sign of the vigor of today's men, of their power . . . of their inventiveness and imagination, and the finest success of their will to modernize the world in all its aspects and in all areas . . . .

Blaise Cendrars,
Advertising Equals Poetry, 1927.

4-1 *Poster by Robert Bereny of Hungary, around 1928, for Cordiatic.*

In France the counterpart of Germany's "utilitarian" art was called *l'art publicitaire*, and it, too, took off after the First World War. Throughout the 1920s French advertising design developed, and by 1933 (the year the Bauhaus closed in Germany) French graphic design was flourishing. A Parisian critic could write: "Advertising, which ten years ago was still despised, is today the undisputed queen of modern business life."[1] The imagination, invention, good taste and skill of the French poster artists placed the artists on the same level as serious artists in the eyes of many of their contemporaries—and in their own eyes.

One of the best was Jean Carlu (Figure 4-2). He was only eighteen in 1918 when he won first prize in a poster competition for toothpaste. He received the prize in a hospital. After working all night to meet the deadline, Carlu had delivered his poster in the morning, and, rushing afterwards to his job, he slipped and fell under a streetcar. His right arm was severed. Unable to manipulate a T-square and triangle, Carlu abandoned his inten-

Industrialists, have your advertising done by poets as Moscow does its propaganda.

Blaise Cendrars,
Advertising Equals Poetry, 1927.

tion to become an architect, and trained himself to draw with his left hand.

Carlu was a student of painting, and in his commercial work he consciously applied techniques from cubism and from traditional theories of proportion—the Golden Section and the *porte d'harmonie*. The Golden Section was the division of squares and rectangles (see Chapter 3), while the *porte d'harmonie* is a peculiar French invention, a formula used in rural French architecture that is based on the relationship of the length of the longest side to the diagonal. Carlu's neighbor in St. Germaine-en-Laye was cubist painter Jean Souverbie, a "fanatic" for cubism, who encouraged Carlu to study the writing of cubist painter Albert Gleizes.[2] Carlu designed an early poster for Phares Marchal (a lighthouse) exactly to the Golden Section. He was, by his own statements, too passionate a believer in the Golden Section when he was young to work another way (Figure 4-3). Throughout his life Carlu was close to other painters, especially Leger and Dufy, and later, to the Surrealists.

Carlu's Funny Little Man appeared in a successful poster for the newspaper *Paris Soir* (Plate C-5). This design, with its flying FLM, evolved from Carlu's study of Gleizes, who taught that every work must be self-sufficient as an organism, and self-contained. It had to be rhythmic in a geometric way—whether the geometry was apparent or not—because that made it "participate in the universal movement, ruled by similar laws," Carlu explained,[3] in an astonishing echo of the cosmological ordering sought by early theorists of proportion. Carlu theorized extensively about this poster as an embodiment of three principles: idea, dynamism, and movement. The idea was carried by the name of the newspaper, *Paris Soir*, heard in the evening when a faraway newsboy cried it and repeated it; next, the dynamism, suggested by the movement of the cry itself—small type as the name is heard distantly and growing larger as it approaches; and third, the action of the newsboy himself, racing, Carlu said, "*court ventre a terre*" (hell-for-leather), his legs stretched to the maximum. His angular, stylized figure exemplified Carlu's theory that angles caught the eye in a way "amorphous" forms did not.[4]

Carlu had consciously analysed the best method to plant his message "deeply and permanently" in the subconscious of the man or woman in the street. He related his simplicity and his geometric forms in graphic design to the simplicity of other modern artifacts—the reinforced concrete of buildings, the motor cars of Henry Ford. Carlu saw economy as a hallmark of the modern period. "Suaveness and simplicity of line, not sentimental curves

4-2 *Jean Carlu.*

4-3 *Lighthouse poster by Jean Carlu of 1924, based on the Golden Section. © 1992 ARS, New York / ADAGP, Paris.*

and meaningless decoration" were what he praised and achieved in so much of his work.

This *Paris Soir* poster of 1928 was successful in attracting the eye of the passerby, the person much courted by poster artists, whose art hung on the sidewalks, not in the galleries. Serious attention was given to the nature of this important person, the *"passant,"* as part of Parisian life. He strolled through the city, finding the street a more congenial atmosphere than home. This urban idler, or *flaneur*, was at home in the arcades of Paris, a luxurious invention of nineteenth-century industry. The arcades were glass-covered, marble-paneled passageways running through entire neighborhoods, passageways lined with elegant shops. They were illuminated by gaslight, and Parisian smokers and strollers and idlers paraded within them until the early hours of the morning. Later critics analysed the importance of all the city's printed ephemera—posters, signs, notices—to this *flaneur*, commenting that the "signs of business are at least as good a wall ornament as an oil painting is to a bourgeois in his salon . . . the terraces of cafes are the balconies from which he looks down on his household after his work is done."[5] With the rebuilding of Paris by Haussmann, wide pavements and boulevards replaced the arcades as promenades, but the tradition of a cafe culture, where anyone with leisure could pass the time sipping, smoking, conversing, idly scanning posters while being entertained by the passing parade, came out of that earlier *flanerie* in a way that is specifically French, and mattered a great deal to the growth of its poster art. Toward the end of the nineteenth century a French law was passed that abolished regulations on public notices, permitting complete liberty in plastering posters on every available surface. Business organizations devoted to "bill-posting," employed an army of workers who could set out and in one day cover the city with posters. The available spaces—walls, fences, and special "billboards" to hold posters—could be covered quickly when a new poster design was launched .[6]

The street as an "interior" for a sauntering crowd of *passants* affected the practices of French poster artists, who decided that a simplified, abstracted figure was easiest to remember from a brief glimpse. Carlu followed a principle of the older, and very successful poster artist Leonetto Cappiello, who isolated a figure against a solid background (light against a dark ground, or dark against a light ground) for a quick impact. Carlu advocated simplification, saying that it was indispensable for the artist whose work had to be comprehended in "the blink of an eye."[7]

4-4 *Poster by Jean Carlu, 1932, Journees d'Esperance or "Days of Hope." © 1992 ARS, New York / ADAGP, Paris.*

4-5 *Poster by Jean Carlu, 1932, L'Obole (the Contribution). An appeal for the blind. © 1992 ARS, New York / ADAGP, Paris.*

A figure like the *Paris Soir* newsboy translated the German FLM into French while keeping many of the original FLM characteristics. Its central figure, flying, fleeting, was as transitory as the paper poster itself. The same qualities of childlikeness are here, along with the geniality of the product salesman. Being French, however, Carlu once reinterpreted the FLM icon as a Funny Little Woman, in a neon-lit poster for electric cooking. Similar treatment of the figure—the circular head, the angled arms and torso, the tilted body, the lack of legs, the simple expression—qualified this as his Funny Little Femme.

His commitment to "put graphic art in the service of peace"[8] was a second way in which Carlu was a spiritual brother to the *gebrauchsgraphikers* of Munich and Berlin. In 1932 he founded the *Office de Propagande Graphique pour la Paix*, marshaling his skills and those of his colleagues against war, racism, oppression, and especially Nazism. Because of Carlu's energy, enthusiasm, and popularity, he spurred the formation of similar organizations in England, Belgium, Spain, Portugal, and Canada. Contemporary critics of the graphic arts envisioned a great tide of publicity for "peace in our time" sweeping across the world.

Carlu's work for causes in the Office of Graphic Propaganda for Peace took completely different styles from that of his commercial work. He used stunning photographs in montage, or he combined photographs with drawings in an ethereal manner. His poster for disarmament caused a scandal when it was exhibited in 1932. Suspended from a red beam, it was thought to be a political statement—a demonstration of rebellion that Carlu never intended.

In an appeal for "days of hope" (Figure 4-4) and for fundraising for blinded war veterans (Figure 4-5) Carlu combined photographs with a white ghostly line. These posters appealed to universal emotions. They touch the viewer's compassion; they appeal to pity. The purity, nobility, and immobility of these whitened profiles resemble marble portrait busts. In these classical statue heads Carlu intuitively reached for an image to correspond to the profound subject matter: the hope of peace, and the tragedy of blindness. These are posters of Greek tragic actors.

The photomontage Carlu used in *La Dette* (Figure 4-6) paired a face disfigured by war wounds with a normal face, combining dark and light sides for a shock of the grotesque. But these faces were not fantasy—bombs and gas and battlefield surgery of the First World War had produced a population of "bashed-in

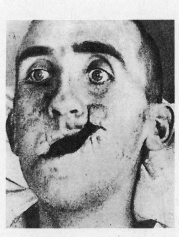

4-6 Poster by Jean Carlu, 1932, La Dette . An appeal for disfigured and crippled veterans. © 1992 ARS, New York / ADAGP, Paris.

4-7 Picture of soldier in army hospital after World War I taken by German war photographer.

faces," "blinded veterans," and "crushed wings" referred to in the poster's text. The photograph Carlu used is similar to the images of mutilated soldiers taken by war photographers (Figure 4-7). Both German and French artists were horrified at the random damage of war, which deformed human anatomy and destroyed normal structure and proportion.

In *La Dette* Carlu transformed a stark documentary photograph into a design by placing the image on a grid constructed vertically of thirds and horizontally of fourths. The light section against the darker, and the lighter face against the void, demonstrates Carlu's technique of light–dark contrast that he learned from Capiello.

With his tremendous artistic awareness, Carlu worked out a personal philosophy of poster art, creating what he called "graphic signs" to accomplish his intention of making a "swift entrance into the soul of the hurrying passer-by."[9] This gifted artist intuitively turned to classical or realistic images to elicit responses of empathy and horror, and when amusement was hoped for, he created new forms.

4-8 *A. M. Cassandre.*

. . . one of the great masters of the street in Paris. I mean Cassandre, who is not only a painter but also one of the most vibrant masters of ceremonies of modern life; a czar of tastes and fashions whose commands are written on posters; a worker and a creator; an inventor who has designed automobile bodies, a new alphabet, a thousand accessories for the printed page, an airplane, and whose signature is worn on the hip unbeknownst by every elegant woman who walks past.

Blaise Cendrars,
1933, on a performance at the Theatre de l'Athenee with sets and costumes by Cassandre.

Cassandre's Unique Little Man

Another Gallicized version of the FLM was invented by the great Cassandre (Adolphe Mouron) (Figure 4-8). In 1932 Cassandre's three-part poster for Dubonnet wine appeared on billboards of Paris (Plate C-6). This triptych showed a funny-looking little man, seated at a cafe table, who acted out a cinematic performance in three scenes. First he regarded his glass of wine, second he tasted it, and third, satisfied, he refilled his glass. The sense of progress through time is enhanced by the coloring of this figure. In the first panel his head and arm and the first letter of the word "Dubonnet" are filled; the rest is outlined. In the second panel the chair, the head and arm, and more of the torso are filled, as well as the "Dubon" of the title. In the last panel the entire figure is colored, and the name of the wine, "Dubonnet," is completely colored, along with the subordinate words. The poster is complete.

This sense of movement recalls Jean Carlu's crier for the *Paris Soir* newspaper, where the letters grew larger to suggest the sound of the approaching newsboy. Cassandre's poster also developed a pun that was already used by the French. The word "Dubonnet" was popularly coupled with the words *du bon* , or, "[some] good"; therefore, *du bon Dubonnet* meant "some good Dubonnet." Cassandre added "Dubo," which sounded like the words *du beau*, or "something beautiful." This animated story, the comic strip of the Dubonnet man, became popular.

The color intensity of the poster increased from the first panel to the third. The pale ochre of the first panel became a sun-bright yellow in the third, warming the face, wine, and hand of the FLM. Originally the figure in the middle panel was set against a blue gray background, but in the posted version the backgrounds were all light. The progressive heightening of the color emphasized the passing of time.

Because it was to be seen in the street, Cassandre felt that the poster must relate to architectural masses. It covered facades; it was pasted on areas of stone and concrete, large, impersonal, bare urban areas. This architectural mating required that the poster be constructed along architectural principles; hence Cassandre's use of the module. The module came from the ancients; in classical buildings it was derived from half the diameter of the column. Using the Golden Section, the *porte d'harmonie*, or the module with regulating lines gave Cassandre's posters a foundation, as a building had a foundation. He stated that the key to his system was to find the module, then use it, then repeat it, giving rhythm to the whole composition.

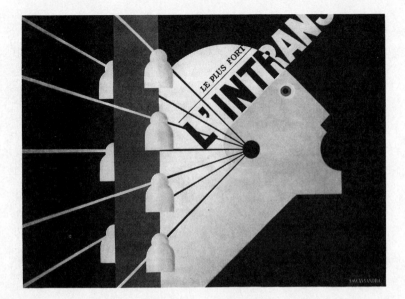

Cassandre's Dubonnet FLM was constructed; it was composed of circles, right angles, and straight lines, resulting from the study of principles of harmony that he had developed. Cassandre's earlier posters for the evening newspaper *L'Intransigeant* and for *Pivolo* wine were similarly constructed. In both he laid down a geometrical structure underneath the pictorial element, inventing a new grid for each poster. In *L'Intransigeant* (Figure 4-9) all the elements in the head of the screaming figure coincide with points on the grid where lines intersect, or where a module is placed. Here Cassandre's composition consisted of two squares, three modules on the base and side. They overlap, making a rectangle of four modules along the base, and three modules on the height. Diagonal lines connect the corners of the squares. The rectangle is also bisected horizontally at the midpoint. Three perfect circles form the ear, the eye, and the open mouth. Their position, and the base of the nose and the length of the chin, are determined by the module. There is such a strong geometrical structure to this poster that it is visible to the naked eye; it actually creates the forms of the head.

It was in his poster for Pivolo wine that Cassandre used the Golden Section for the first time (Figure 4-10). All the parts of the bird—the *pie*, or magpie, of "Pievolo"—and the width of the wineglass, the placement of the name, and the depth of the bottom border are determined by the square, its section, the angles formed by the regulating lines, and the circles formed by a compass on certain points placed within modules, or divisions of modules.[10] The bird's head, wing, and eye are located on these points.

By 1926, when he was twenty-five, Cassandre formed his theory of the poster. It evolved from his own dual artistic directions. On the one hand, he was a painter; on the other, he earned a living making posters. He even adopted his pseudonym, "Cassandre" for commercial art in order that his real name could be reserved until he became a full time painter. The duality of his artistic life caused Cassandre to brood on the exact difference between fine and commercial art more than his colleagues did. This duality was apparent in his working methods at his studio.

Visitors to Cassandre's modern villa in Versailles were surprised to find that he worked with the tools of the architect—compass, ruler, T-squares. His studio was what he called a *usine à affiches*—a "poster factory."[11] To him the poster was a mass-produced object, no different from a fountain pen or an automobile. Cassandre's utilitarian approach allies his thought with the Bauhaus masters, but he arrived independently at his views of the mechanical nature of the poster.[12] Cassandre knew the poster was for business, and a part of marketing, intended for "strictly material needs," as he put it. His clients owned newspapers, steamships, railroads, vineyards, and factories. He worked well with them. He could say of his poster: "It must have a commercial function."[13] Cassandre's acceptance of the business reality affecting his art work did not mean that he took his commercial work less seriously than his painting. He believed posters to be halfway between the cinema and painting; they were film animated by color. Cassandre loved cinema and admired films of Abel Gance, René Clair, and Sergei Eisenstein.

Cassandre believed that the poster artist communicated with the masses in the same way that the medieval illustrators, Greek potters, or fresco painters of ancient Egypt did—anonymously. For Cassandre the poster artist should be faceless. He or she should be an unknown worker, like the craftsmen of the Middle Ages and antiquity. Poster art, Cassandre felt, moved toward the collective and anonymous. Traces of personality, quirks of character, were to be obliterated. Pure and poetic individualism and lyricism were for painting and in its process eternal elements might be discovered. For this reason he loved Cubism, finding in it a "relentless logic" that replaced the "warped" vision of Impressionist painting.

Ironically, Cassandre's posters are infused with his unique sensibility. His manner of combining a strong supporting foundation with delicate illustration is unique. But he continued to insist that the poster demanded utter resignation on the part of the artist. "He must not asert his personality."[14] Cassandre insisted that the poster maker act like a telegraph official: "he did not initiate news, he spread it." "He is only required to bring about a clear, good and exact connection." In the same breath Cassandre made the odd statement that the poster artist might, in spite of himself, send a message with the "impress of his own fear."[15]

Cassandre's posters, though imbued with architectural elements and the logic of cubist painting, angered his contemporary, the architect and painter Le Corbusier. When *Au Bucheron*, Cassandre's first poster, caused a sensation on the streets, Cassandre was attacked in Le Corbusier's publication *l' Esprit Nouveau*. "There is tumult in the streets . . . . In ten days Cubism has blossomed over a kilometer—a display for the masses. The masses take it in and are amused. But there is nothing amusing about this particular Cubism. It is a fake, a crude mark-down of serious work (is Leger rejoicing in or deploring this development?) a formula purloined and massacred by a dauber."[16] Cubism did not belong to the masses, in Le Corbusier's view.

This tirade against Cassandre reveals once again the jealous defenses fine art asserted against commercial art. No one more sincere, more talented, more sensitive than Casssandre could be found. Yet because his work was seen by the public, the "masses," it brought derision from a leading modernist architect and painter.[17]

The *rue-spectacle*, the theater of the streets of Paris, included the poster. More traffic and more commerce made the city streets hectic and crowded. A change had occurred since the *flaneur* strolled idly through the arcades after midnight. Fernand Leger, the painter friend of both Carlu and Cassandre, found the streets *too* dynamic. They shattered and wrecked his nerves. Real life had become so stressful that contrast was needed. And what part did the poster play in the show? The posters should be calming, not vibrating, Leger said. In a debate on the street scene,[18] Leger cited the flatness and verticality of Cassandre's posters as advantages. Because of those properties, the poster did not become a hole in the facade. They fit Leger's demand for a harmonious orchestration of all the elements in the street scene, rather than a jazz performance with many solo parts. Leger advocated a visual order of the street so that the nerves of the modern passerby would be soothed. He visualized a "landscape"—and asked why beautiful posters like Cassandre's should not be part of the landscape. Unlike Le Corbusier, who ridiculed the "dauber," Leger specifically praised the "art poster" of Cassandre. Both modernists grappled with the question of the urban mess; Leger to orchestrate its diversity, Le Corbusier to construct holding pens for its masses.[19]

The FLM Travels Through Europe

Outside France,[20] spontaneous eruptions of funny little men appeared in ads. In Italy, Onorato Pupazzi created one who shared with so many other FLMs the formal attire of tux and top hat, flying to an engagement (Figure 4-11). A cheerful bulbous chef appeared in Holland for Biscuit Verklade (Plate C-7).

In Hungary graphic artists designed political and film posters. But a direct contact with German commercial art was cited at the time as the reason for the sudden improvement in quality in the work of Robert Bereny. Bereny had spent the years from 1919 to 1927 in Germany and, returning to Hungary, produced a typical FLM for Cordiatic (Figure 4-1). This poster had a

4-11 *An Italian FLM done for a publisher by Oronato Pupazzi.*

4-12 *Robert Bereny poster for Modiano cigars.*

4-13 *Poster for Hungarian cigarettes by Johann Repeze, 1932.*

We know the marvelous power of agitation . . . . The bourgeoisie knows the power of advertising. The advertisement is industrial, commercial agitation. No business, even the most certain and reliable, keeps going without advertisement. It is the weapon which is born of competition . . . . We cannot leave this weapon, this agitation on behalf of trade, in the hands . . . of the bourgeois foreigners trading here. Everything in the U.S.S.R. must work for the benefit of the proletariat. Give advertising some thought!

Vladimir Mayakovsky, 1923.

4-14 *Vladimir Mayakovsky and Alexander Rodchenko for the Soviet State department store GUM. It reads "A person cannot go without a watch. The only clocks and watches to have are Mozers. Mozers can only be bought at GUM." Moscow, 1923. © Estate of A. Rodchenko/VAGA, New York 1993.*

"positively explosive" effect, according to the press of the time.[21] Its conception and execution were praised as fresh and new. Robert Bereny's posters of 1929 are filled with FLM figures (Figure 4-12), so it seems that in his years in Germany, Bereny had adopted its prevailing sales motif. The artist saw himself as using a "naked schematic language of signs"[22]—the FLM had become the recognized sign of the salesman. Another Hungarian FLM was used by Johann Repcze (Figure 4-13), associated as the FLM often was, with tobacco. In London Austin Cooper anglicized the FLM in posters for the Underground.

Early "Socialist Graphic Design"

After the First World War the Soviet Union needed to strengthen its shaky political position and to communicate with its majority population of illiterates. To accomplish these goals, the state enlisted both fine and graphic artists into its service. Artist Alexander Rodchenko and playwright Vladimir Mayokovsky invented "production art," the Russian equivalent of the German *gebrauschgraphik* and the French *publicité*. As avant-garde artists they enthusiastically attacked new problems, creating images for a new society, its products and its social projects (Figure 4-14). With whole-hearted fervor for the new industrial state, Rodchenko even wore a self-designed uniform, or "production dress," at work. In advertising collaborations the two titled themselves "Advertisement-Constructor Mayakovsky-Rodchenko." They operated out of their apartments in downtown Moscow.

During the years 1923 to 1925 the "socialist designer" had the state as his client. One project found Mayakovsky writing poems and drawing illustrations for caramel wrappers to send political messages to peasants and soldiers. These bright, red-starred cartoons depicted incidents in the Red Army victory over the Whites. For the Soviet state campaign against illiteracy Mayakovsky invented the slogan "the source of knowledge and light," which became the centerpiece for a massive campaign to market, display and sell books. It included designs for hats for book clerks and book kiosks for the streets.

Mayakovsky and Rodchenko were exemplary in their loyal and productive service to the state. Others who had been in fine arts—making the scorned "landscaping and still-life" of the old order—converted to the new idealistic purposes of the Soviet state. Even Kandinsky created (in 1923) a trademark for the publishing house Arena (Figure 4-15), and El Lissitsky designed a

4-15 *Vassily Kandinsky, trademark for the Arena publishing house, 1923. © 1992 ARS, New York / ADAGP, Paris*

4-16 *Book cover by El Lissitsky for "Good," 1928.*

Art for the proletariat is not a sacred shrine where they go only for slothful contemplation; it is the labour, the factory, which puts objects of aesthetic quality on the market for all of them.

Nikolai Punin,
Iskusstvo communy #4, (Art of the Commune), 1918.

book cover for Mayakovsky's poem *"Khorosho!"* (Good!) honoring the October revolution (Figure 4-16). Other artists promoted "Soviet" cigarettes from the Leningrad State Tobacco Trust. Only an occasional "reactionary" ornamental illustration appeared for the State Fats Trust, official supplier of cosmetics and perfume. But the vast majority of posters, ads, books, and packaging were amalgams of the practical needs of the state, individual styles, and recent inventions in Constructivism and Suprematism in painting. Ideologue Nikolai Punin remarked in 1919 that "Suprematism has blossomed in luxuriant colours all over Moscow. Sign boards, exhibitions, cafes—everything is Suprematism."[23]

This artistic community illustrated Soviet types. To reach all classes when advertising cigarettes, the designer portrayed the soldier, the worker, the intellectual, the peasant, even a remnant of the despicable bourgeoisie (Figure 4-17). The blouse of the peasant, the uniform of the soldier, and the smock and hammer of the worker identified them, as the briefcase identified the intellectual, and the top hat, evening shoes, gloves and stick marked the remnant of the decadent bourgeoisie. Thus the new classes bore their identifying attributes as the old saints in the cathedrals carried their instruments of martyrdom.

With little contact with the West, and with a patriotic conviction of their unique historical mission, Soviet commercial artists invented their own cast of characters. None looked quite like the capitalist salesman, the FLM of the bourgeois cultures of Germany and France. Political requirements evoked simplified types. These lifelike Soviet representations, which in these early days coexisted with alternative artistic approaches—abstraction,

4-17 *Anonymous poster for "Our Brand" cigarettes, 1925, showing all Russian types smoking the cigarette: the Russian soldier in his uniform, the worker carrying his hammer, the professional with his briefcase, and his wife (not smoking), the peasant in his tunic, and the decadent bourgeois in formal clothes.*

4-18 *Poster promoting subscriptions to the publication "Atheist at the Machine Tool," 1924.*

photography, montage—foreshadowed later Soviet realism. A design of 1924 came closest to the childlike FLM forms in a poster urging subscriptions to the government publication "Atheist at the Machine Tool" (Figure 4-18). Here the small smiling figure with a badge of Lenin on his coat is promoting one of the country's most important products: the letters read "I am an atheist."

CHAPTER 5

The Funny Little Man Is Abstracted

Non-objective painting has left the Museums; non-objective painting is in the street itself, the squares, the towns and the whole world....

ALEXANDER RODCHENKO, MANIFESTO, MOSCOW, 1919

The form is always bound to its time ... since it is nothing more than the means necessary today in which today's revelation manifests itself, resounds.

Wassily Kandinsky,
"On the Problem of Form," 1912.

modern movements in fine arts reached the mass public through the work of commercial artists, who consciously appropriated techniques from modern painting to apply to their work. Frenzel, the great chronicler, examined the modern technique of abstraction, and evaluated it against a realistic style in commercial art.[1] He asserted that a realistic illustration is perfect only when it is absolutely identical with the original (anticipating Baudrillard by some sixty years).[2] Large, realistic scenes full of glamorous figures, or of closeups of clocks or electric refrigerators or pretty faces or Milky Ways or streamlined automobiles, made no lasting impression because there was so much visual "talk" that the product was forgotten.[3] In magazines these closely packed ad pages canceled each other. Though each might be well-drawn and large, the magazine context neutralized each realistic presentation.

Abstraction suggested content powerfully. Cassandre's notorious poster *L'Intransigeant* (see Figure 4-9) was considered an exemplary abstract poster, one that successfully synthesized form and content. Designers were swept up in the success of this application of the new methods mastered by Cassandre. His design, because it departed from realism, aroused the curiosity of the passerby, the much-courted time-pressed urbanite. Because the details were missing, the viewer was forced to study the poster,

5-1 *Trademark by Karl Schulpig for a German coal company, 1924.*

5-2 *Zietara's mark for the George Hemmeter brewery in Munich, 1921.*

5-3 *Mark by Karl Schulpig for the Bolle dairy, 1923.*

5-4 *Schulpig's Trademark for a maker of musical instruments, 1923.*

5-5 *Schulpig's trademark for a manufacturer of adding machines, 1923.*

5-6 *Hermann Virl's mark for a gingerbread baker, 1922.*

piecing it together. Frenzel reasoned that such mental effort caused the poster to plant itself in the viewer's mind. For advertising, that was success.

Narrative illustrations resembled a rambling story that digressed into anecdote and biography but was quickly forgotten. In abstraction, the form became more concentrated as it became smaller. The more concentrated , the more effective—the smaller the better. Much commercial art of this period was designed for the small spaces of newspaper ads, business cards,

5-7 *A mark for an association of industries by Konrad Jochheim, 1927.*

5-8 *Karl Schulpig's mark for a chemical company, 1921.*

5-9 *Design for a glass maker's ad by Karl Schulpig, Berlin, 1925.*

5-10 *Trademark by Dore Monkemeyer-Corty, 1930.*

letterheads—what the Germans referred to as *Kleingraphik*—rather than for large poster areas. The ultimate reduction to the smallest and most concentrated form for publicity was the trademark.

Trademarks using the FLM appeared early in Zietara's work for a Munich brewery (Figure 5-2). The 1920s saw FLMs representing coal (Figure 5-1), a dairy (Figure 5-3), musical instruments (Figure 5-4), adding machines (Figure 5-5), and a gingerbread baker (Figure 5-6). He appeared for industrial enterprises (Figure 5-7), a chemical company (Figure 5-8), and glass (Figure 5-9). These trademarks were the specialty of designers Karl Schulpig, Konrad Jochheim, and Dore Monkemeyer-Corty. Designs by Dora Corty were noted for imaginative treatment of little human forms (Figure 5-10). Fred Hendriok specialized in

5-11 *Mark by Fred Hendriok, c. 1929.*

5-12 *Mark by Fred Hendriok, c. 1929.*

5-13 *Dora Corty's realistic style in a poster for milk, 1930.*

5-14 *Dora Corty's abstract style in a poster for milk, 1930.*

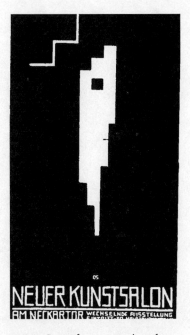

5-15 *Poster for a new salon of art by Oskar Schlemmer, 1919.*

5-16 *Poster by Otto Dix for an art exhibit, 1919.*

trademarks of exceedingly compressed little men that contemporaries admired as especially pleasing (Figures 5-11 and 5-12).[4] Corty could work in both realistic and abstract styles, as shown in her two 1930 ads for milk (Figures 5-13 and 5-14).

The FLM icon was inherently adaptable to the technique of abstraction. It was small to begin with. Further miniaturization added the force of compression. The icon was already halfway to abstraction; the FLM's feet and hands had been simplified and reduced to shapes.

The circle had long been recognized as a sign for a human head, so to use the perfect sphere for a head was a logical design step in making trademarks. Cylinders, rectangles, and angles formed other parts. The essential features of the FLM coincided with the geometrizing tendency of early modernism.

The powerful concept of abstraction was so important to modernists that some saw it as leading toward the discovery of a "new law of identification"[5] in art. Experiments in abstracting the human figure had already begun in modern design. Oskar Schlemmer had reduced the human head to planes and lines for an art poster (Figure 5-15). In the 1922 seal he designed later for the Bauhaus he constructed a head of lines and planes, arranged in a circle (Figure 1-18). The signet appeared on its booklets, posters and letterheads, signalling, through these geometric forms, the position of the Bauhaus as a modernist enterprise. Here elemental planes and lines, spatially contained, and reduced in complexity, translated cubism into graphic design.

Expressionists used geometric forms at the same period, and for a similar purpose, but to convey different states of mind. Such poster artists as Dorothea Maetzel-Johannsen, Emil Maetzel, and Otto Dix (Figure 5-16) created angular little humans in woodcut technique. Significantly, their creatures announce art exhibits; their angular bodies, contorted expressions, and "ugly" faces are acceptable there. But in the business world of commercial posters, the figure had to be appealing, an FLM figure complete with its humorous and ingratiating qualities.

Theories of Modern Art in Publicity

Early graphic designers believed themselves to be operating within the same sphere of ideas as painters and sculptors. During the 20s and 30s both "high" and "low" artists believed themselves to be part of a revolution in modern art movements—Cubism, Expressionism, Futurism. One goal of modernism, to

How does a horse see the world, how does an eagle, a doe, or a dog? It is a poverty-stricken convention to place animals into landscapes as seen by men; instead, we should contemplate the soul of the animal to divine its way of sight . . . .

Expressionist painter Franz Marc, 1920.

. . . the science of design consists in instituting relations between straight lines and curves . . . A picture which contained only straight lines or only curves would not express life . . . .

Albert Gleizes, Cubism, 1912.

We will glorify war—the only true hygiene of the world—militarism, patriotism, the destructive gesture of anarchist, the beautiful ideas which kill, and the scorn of woman . . . . We will destroy museums, libraries, and fight against moralism, feminism, and all utilitarian cowardice . . . .

F. T. Marinetti, "The Foundation and Manifesto of Futurism," 1908.

obliterate the line between fine and applied art, was for designers a practical reality. Commercial artists never considered themselves to be anything but complete moderns.

No one pursued the theoretical more seriously than Jean Carlu. His statements about the aesthetic of the poster[6] follow from his assertion that the poster must be a work of art. Carlu assumed that art work done for graphic and "propaganda" purposes[7] obeyed the same aesthetic laws governing *all* art. Under the influence of his mentor Gleizes, Carlu accepted Plato's statement that the artist must make use of forms to express the "movements of the soul." All artists gave visual and concrete expressions to feelings. That was the purpose of visual art.

Carlu then argued that the reason for art was that human beings needed to externalize their feelings. Although smiles and tears were primitive expressions of such feelings, the poet expressed feelings in an art form. The visual artist was a poet— "the artist must be moved in order to move others," Carlu said. Nature rested on a geometric base, recognized by all human beings. Lines appealed to the emotions; curved lines touched something fundamental, something associated with laughter.

Here Carlu followed his mentor, Gleizes, whose important book on Cubism he read in his teens.[8] Gleizes, with his circle— Leger, Duchamp, the critic Apollinaire and others—advanced abstract painting beyond Cubism into pure realms of intellectual speculation. It was Gleizes who separated the artist from "most people"[9]—those who wandered around the world blind to the Platonic forms hidden under the surface. Gleizes isolated the artist as the only human who could discern the underlying forms, which verified preexisting ideas.[10] This gave Cubism its special importance. It was not superficial like Impressionism, which painted surface colors and light. Cubism was the art closest to true nature. Nature was its inspiration, for in it the artist beheld the form that matched the preexisting idea. The artist endeavored to "enclose" the quality of this form in a symbol likely to impress others. Seeing painting as a kind of power, Gleizes maintained that the painter forced the crowd to assume an attitude toward his or her painting that the artist assumed before nature.

This power of forms functioned in the poster, Carlu said. If its images were exceedingly potent, they could bypass reason and penetrate the sensibility of the spectator. Thus, the spectator remembered the image. Also, the spectator would associate the name of the "propagandist" (the product) with this strong visual memory, thus achieving what Carlu and others worried about so much—the brief moment they had to impress the busy citydweller.

Gleizes and Carlu rejected what they called "amorphous" forms, those based on imitation instead of abstraction. To illustrate this crucial point Carlu compared a schematic drawing of his *Paris Soir* newsboy poster with a new drawing made of the same subject.[11] Nothing could illustrate his thoughts more clearly (Figure 5-17). He calls the new drawing "non-limited," or amorphous. Its proportions, the shading of the volumes, the street scene with its lamps and windowed buildings, the details of the neckerchief, all simulate realism. The man even has a patch on one rumpled trouser leg. His open mouth implies the sound of the newsboy's cry.

Carlu diagrammed the preferred abstract and "limited" composition that he had actually used In the successful *Paris Soir* poster (Plate C-5). What had disappeared? First, gone were all the real objects of a city street. Only a light spot—the newsboy—remained on the dark background. This followed the dark and light theories of Leonetti Cappiello's, which Carlu accepted.[12] Most significantly, the figure of the newsboy had metamorphosed into a dynamic flying form, the legs compressed into one shape, the arms into another, strong angles enclosing the sphere of the head. Minimal lines indicate the fingers and cap. Most important, the round hole of the mouth, the source of the cry "Paris Soir," which Carlu had enlarged as the sound approached,

5-17 *Two drawings by Jean Carlu to explain his philosophy of "amorphous" and abstract forms based on his successful poster,* Paris Soir, *in the publication* Arts et Metiers Graphique, *1928.*

The Venus de Milo is a graphic example of decline. It is not a real woman, but a parody. Angelo's David is a deformation . . . .

Kazimir Malevich,
1915.

The concepts of "pure science" "pure art," "independent truth and beauty" are alien to us. We are practitioners—and in this lies the distinctive feature of our cultural consciousness.

Ossip Brik,
From Pictures to Textile Prints, 1924.

Not only the poster, but also the picture, the statue—in less volatile forms and with more profound ideas, stronger feelings—can emerge as graphic aids to the assimilation of Communist truth.

Analotii Lunacharsky,
People's Commissar for Enlightenment,
1920–22.

became the whole point of the poster. Through digressions into scenery, windows, lamps, and patches, the inferior version, the first sketch, missed this opportunity to streak into the spectator's mind.

The successful version of the *Paris Soir* poster is what Carlu described as a "closed composition, rhythmic and based on a geometric system." The closed composition, unlike the first sketch, is not interrupted by the lamppost, or cut off at the knees. It is an entity, potent and rhythmic, in the spatial arrangement of image and type and the counterpoint of the arms and legs. Though its parts had similar shapes, they differed in dimension, an important point to Gleizes and Carlu. The angles also differed, but echoed each other.

Carlu put the emotional power of the poster into the service of commerce. He located the commercial poster in a larger context, as a part of the modern world. Idealistically, Carlu expressed the power of the poster artist to relieve the burdens of the "modern soul" by combining the spontaneous line, the "issue of the purest feeling," with the geometric forms, "the skeleton supporting the muscles, nervous system, circulation, and all that is life."[13]

Such goals for commercial art seem amazingly ambitious today, but they verify that early commercial artists associated themselves, no less than architects and painters, with the hopeful atmosphere of the 1920s, when the rejection of the immediate past, with its wars and suffering, permeated people's thoughts. Commercial artists manned the drawing boards in Carlu's organization, the Office of Graphic Propaganda for Peace[14], and prepared to combat evil with T-squares. Pure abstraction was a weapon; geometric forms were its bullets.

Soviet Abstraction and the New State

After the Revolution of 1917, artists of the new Soviet state adopted abstraction as the appropriate formal expression of the new order. The seeds of abstraction were already there, planted before the outbreak of the First World War. Cubism developed in Paris after 1905, De Stijl in Holland around 1917, Futurism in Italy by 1909, Synchronism in America in 1912. Two Russian merchant collectors[15] had purchased hundreds of paintings by Picasso, Matisse and other moderns and brought them to Moscow before the outbreak of the First World War. The Futurist painter Filippo Marinetti had visited Russia in 1914. Russian

The square is a living, regal infant.

Kazimir Malevich,
1915.

Malevich came up to me and said: You are the only painter here, but do you know what you are doing?

I don't know.

Do you know that everything they're doing . . . has already been seen and done: It's all out of date. Now there is something new in the air, something closer to ourselves, something more typically Russian. That's what I'm working on myself and I can see it in your work already, intuitively, I can feel it's there!

Malelvich to Rodchenko,
1916.

painter Kasimir Malevich was affected by Cubist, Fauvist, and Futurist ideas, formulating his own abstract style called Suprematism. Another Russian artist, Vladimir Tatlin, constructed the first completely abstract relief sculpture, composed of glass and wood shapes, early in the formation of a movement eventually called Constructivism. Both Constructivism and Suprematism rejected representation and any imitation of the real world in favor of purely imagined abstract forms, appropriate to the new age of the machine and mass production.

Just as their political leaders rejected the social structures of the past, Russian commercial artists rejected the baggage of realistic art. Abstract art seemed the aesthetic equivalent of revolutionary socialism, and it was embraced as the appropriate style of the proletariat. Malevich became a professor at the art academy in Moscow, a recognition of the official sanction of abstraction.

The same impulse to unify the fine and applied arts that had created the Bauhaus inspired a new school in Moscow. In 1918 the Moscow Institute of Painting, Sculpture and Architecture merged with the Stroganov Art School to become the Free Art Studios, later renamed Vkhutemas from the initials of its formal name.[16] Alexander Rodchenko directed its enthusiastic staff in developing theoretical and pedagogical approaches to the new profession of socialist designer. Courses included stage design, poster design, architecture, textile design, ceramics, typography, and graphic design. The Moscow art school, like the Bauhaus, envisioned itself as transforming society through design, shaping industrially produced products for the masses.

The Politics of Geometry

Rodchenko viewed "construction," or constructivist design, as the natural manifestation of contemporary consciousness, a consciousness formed by industry.[17] At the Vkhutemas instructors specified that objects be made with economy of means and be based on the principles of the straight line and the geometrically constructed curve (Figure 5-18). As at the Bauhaus, the Vkhutemas instructors emphasized the integrity of materials and the relationship between form, function, structure, and materials. The concepts of *funktsionalnost* (functionality) and *tselesoobraznost* (the coincidence of form with purpose) were central to Vkhutemas teaching. As modernists, they rejected ornament, decoration, added flourishes. Geometric forms of the square, the circle, and the triangle were universal forms that they believed

5-18 *Constructivist Design for a logo for the publishers Krug.*

5-19 *Covers by Rodchenko for Lef, "Left Front of the Arts," 1923–25.*

belonged to all classes of people, and were therefore appropriate to the Soviet state.

Between 1923 and 1925, Rodchenko and Mayakovsky, calling themselves *Reklam-konstruktor*, or advertising constructors, created "about fifty posters, one hundred signs, wrapping papers, dust covers, wrappers, illuminated signs, advertisement drums, illustrations in magazines and papers . . . ."[18] After 1921 Rodchenko's art was almost exclusively in typography, photography, and design for socialist purposes.

Rodchenko was the principal designer for the periodical *LEF* (Left Front of the Arts) from 1923 to 1925, while the poet Mayakovsky was its editor (Figure 5-19). Graphic designs for *LEF* and for books and book covers set the style for "constructivist" typography. This style, still an influence in graphic design, resulted from three principles ruling Rodchenko's life: the political convictions of revolutionary socialism, the theoretical principles of fine arts, and the practical mechanics of printing. The look of *LEF* was rough and rude, a deliberate political rejection of the fine printing of prerevolutionary society. Crudeness was a virtue; plain, coarse, honest design stood for the new, just society that demanded the "de-aestheticizing"of produced objects. And the collaborative effort printing required was preferred to the isolated individual artist in the studio. In his paintings Rodchenko had previously eliminated all but the plane and the line; in his graphic design, planes and lines appear as inked bars ordering the spatial surface of the page. His sculptures, slabs of rough wood named "Spatial Constructions,"were the three-dimensional equivalent of the *LEF* covers.

The practical exigencies of letterpress printing affected its look. Working directly with the bed of the press influenced the design—locking up type in forms mandated a strong horizontal and vertical composition, evident in *LEF's* first covers. Two color printing was the cheapest kind—and poverty was a virtue. Masking the large sans serif types caused half the face to print in the first color in the first run, the other half to print in the second color in the second run. The concept of "faktura," or the evident handling of the material, which Rodchenko and other constructivists investigated, is apparent in the intervention of his hand in altering, masking, bisecting, and otherwise manipulating type, and allowing the wooden grain of press furniture to print.

The Vkhutemas and the Bauhaus

Both the Russian school and the Bauhaus existed during the same period; the Vkhutemas closed in 1930 as the Bauhaus struggled to its death. Students gravitated to the Vkhutemas as to the Bauhaus because they heard that great avant-garde artists were teaching a revolutionary curriculum there. "Work for LIFE and not for PALACES, TEMPLES, CEMETERIES AND MUSEUMS," Rodchenko directed students at the Vkhutemas.

Rodchenko's class was called "construction," and he was named its "construction leader." Students were surprised to see him enter the classroom dressed like a pilot—military jacket, boots, leggings, and cap—though he did not sport goggles as did the constructivist architect Alexei Gans. Like other moderns he was attracted to aviation. For them the airplane was a metaphor for modernism; it stood for speed, technology, the machine (Figure 5-20). Rodchenko's clothing—beige, black and gray in

5-20 *Designs of logos with airplanes by Rodchenko in Lef, 1923. © Estate of A. Rodchenko/VAGA, New York 1993.*

5-21 *Design by Rodchenko and Mayakovsky for "Resinotrust" pacifiers. © Estate of A. Rodchenko/ VAGA, New York 1993.*

contrasting matte and shiny fabrics—matched the still lifes he arranged for his students. Several students executed commissions that Rodchenko and Mayakovsky received. After classes they would return to Rodchenko's large apartment, a gift of the government, to work. The method was brisk, economical, modern. Rodchenko would telephone Mayakovsky for the text of a new poster. As they spoke, Rodchenko would start to sketch in black, blue, and red crayons on graph paper that he kept ready on his desk. He worked quickly, rarely making corrections, tossing the sketch to the student assistants with a few remarks about color. Students left, worked through the night, and delivered the completed poster the next morning. There was rarely any alteration, and the posters were printed the same day.[19]

One such poster, executed by students with a text from Mayakovsky, caused criticism (Figure 5-21). Mayakovsky wrote for a poster advertising baby pacifiers, "Ready to suck till old age comes." He defended this poster on social terms, claiming that it was in the interest of a better life—at the time hungry Russian babies were given dirty rags to suck to stop them from crying. To the poet Mayakovsky and the artist Rodchenko, the advertising of factory-made clean rubber pacifiers was noble work. Mayakovsky called this poster, "propaganda in the interest of a healthy generation and for civilization."[20] The pacifier poster, with its large bright geometric shapes, a kind of factory-made FLM, typified the new art. Of such work, a member of their Constructivist circle, literary critic Ossip Brik, wrote, "The propaganda of productional art is being crowned with success."[21]

5-22 *FLM by Rodchenko, saying "Look!," 1924. © Estate of A. Rodchenko/VAGA, New York 1993.*

5-23 *FLM by Rodchenko with "The Latest News, 1924". © Estate of A. Rodchenko/VAGA, New York 1993.*

5-24 *FLM by Rodchenko, with bell, announcing "A New Item," 1924. © Estate of A. Rodchenko/VAGA, New York 1993.*

The poster is not a painting but a "machine for announcing."

A. M. Cassandre,
L'art Internationale d'aujourd'hui, 1929.

5-25 *Rodchenko's poster for the Leningrad State Publishers, saying "Books in all branches of Knowledge," 1925. It was never printed. © Estate of A. Rodchenko/VAGA, New York 1993.*

Rodchenko created several abstract FLMs. A little figure announced new books: "Today's latest" (Figures 5-22 and 5-23). In the figure with the clanging bell (Figure 5-24) Rodchenko depicts what these graphic salesmen so often did: announce. Cassandre had maintained that the poster is not a painting but a modern *"machine à annoncer"*[22] and often there was some attempt at representing sound, crying the event as Carlu had in the *Paris Soir* poster. Rodchenko's poster for "Books" (Figure 5-25) should be compared to Cassandre's *L'Intransigeant* (Figure 4-9) for different treatments of the same intention.

It was Rodchenko's colleague and wife, Varvara Stepanova, who explicitly stated the goal of introducing sound into graphics. Varvara Stepanova was one of the leading figures of the Russian avant-garde movement, who played a central part in developing fine and applied arts in relation to the Socialist state (Figure 5-26). From the first optimistic revolutionary days, through the policy changes of the 30s, and during the later Stalinist oppression, Stepanova was prominent in the radical culture of artists and intellectuals. She was a painter, an innovator in poetry, graphics, and all "utilitarian" design.

A believer in the new social structure promised by the Revolution, Stepanova designed for this new world. She believed

5-26 *Self-portrait by Varvara Stepanova. © Estate of V. Stepanova/VAGA, New York 1993.*

5-27 *Drawings, designs for athletes, in the 1923 issue of Lef by Stepanova. © Estate of V. Stepanova/VAGA, New York 1993.*

I am breaking up the dead monotony of interconnected printed letters by means of painterly graphics, and I am advancing toward a new kind of artistic creation.

Varvara Stepanov,
"Concerning My Graphics at the Exhibition", catalog of the "Tenth State Exhibition: Nonobjective Creation and Suprematism," Moscow, 1919.

At present we are living through an unusual period in time a new cosmic creation has become reality in the world a creativity within ourselves which pervades our consciousness.

El Lissitsky,
Moscow, 1920.

that "standardization" was essential. Like Rodchenko, Stepanova advocated "production costumes" for work, and designed uniforms in her own fabrics for the factory worker, the teacher, the professional. She also designed costumes for athletes that formed geometric patterns on the body (Figure 5-27). Her stage sets, too, emphasized functionality and economy, characteristics of modernism and the machine.

At the influential 1919 state exhibition of avant garde art in Moscow, Stepanova described her pieces as "linking the new movement of nonobjective poetry—sounds and letters—with a painterly perception . . . I am advancing toward a new kind of artistic creation. . . I am introducing sound as a new quality in graphic painting."[23] She composed poetry, inventing nonsense words to transcend normal speech in an attempt to reach something universal in sound itself.

Stepanova passionately believed in the new nonobjective art. "It embraced all aspects of art and life itself," she said. Abstraction in the early days after the Soviet revolution was seen as a matter of the spirit—as a rejection of the materialism of modern times that lingered in other painting. For her, nonobjective painting marked the beginning of a great new epoch "destined to open the doors to mysteries more profound than science or technology."[24] Her 1920 painting, *Two Figures at a Table*, was made without the touch of human hands: she constructed its forms with ruler and compass. In it two human beings work at a desk in front of an abstract painting. It seems very much like an abstraction of Stepanova and her companion/husband Rodchenko, who shared an apartment, the same political philosophy, circle of friends, and materials. They were two who defined the Constructivist style in graphic design through their books, posters, and publications.

Constructivist book design emphasized type, large sans serif letters whose bold, structural, undecorated forms accorded with Constructivist principles. Usually huge type filled the page (Figure 5-28). Printer's rules, bars, and other typographic elements added to the constructed, skeletal, rectangular character of the design. When photographs were used they were manipulated as graphic units; repeated, silhouetted, black-bordered, angled. Constructivist graphic design for mass production was signed by the designer, since they were regarded as independent works of art.

Stepanova's later constructivist graphic design changed from its rough, material-conscious look. Thinner type, lower case letters, more white space, more precise relationships between

5-28 Cover for the Constructivist architectural journal Contemporary Architecture by architect Alexei Gans, 1928.

5-29 Cover for first issue of Literature and the Arts, by Stepanova, 1930. © Estate of V. Stepanova/VAGA, New York 1993.

. . . the taste of the masses is formed not only by, say, Pushkin, but also by the pattern of wallpapers and sweet-wrappers.

Pravda,
March 30, 1924.

. . . the picture is dying, it is indissolubly linked with the forms of the capitalist regime, with its cultural ideology.

Ossip Brik,
From Pictures to Textile Prints, 1924.

graphic elements, resulted in a "curvilinear" constructivism by 1930 (Figure 5-29).

National Types in Commercial and Popular Art

Rodchenko claimed that "line has bid a red farewell to painting." But the abstraction he advocated did not totally replace subject matter. Beneath the surface of abstraction a love of representation persisted. Posters publicizing agricultural journals, publishing houses and cigarette factories owned by the state were far from abstract. The state reached the masses by holding the poster up as a mirror: people looking at the poster saw themselves doing what the state wanted them to do. Clear, detailed (though often poorly drawn) illustrations of different social types filled the poster. Signs of class were clear: the cap on the worker, the military uniform of the soldier, the tunic of the peasant and the kerchief of the peasant grandmother. Everything—beards and mustaches, clothing, gestures—added up to reality.

Representational images of the figure persisted elsewhere. The woman in the "Books" poster is a Russian: her kerchief says so. National differences were accepted in graphics of the time. A

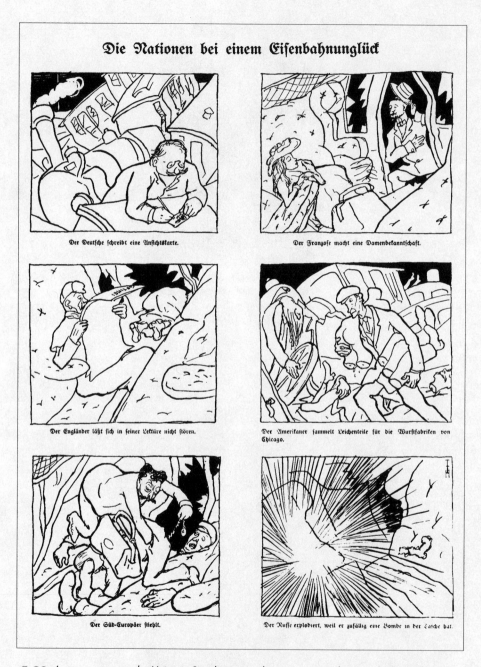

5-30 A pre-war cartoon by Heine in Simplicissimus showing accepted national types. After a train wreck the German keeps writing postcards, the Frenchman flirts with a lady, the Englishman reads his newspaper (The Times) , the American picks up bodies for the meat factories of Chicago, the Mediterranean steals, and the Russian blows up because he was a revolutionary and the bomb in his pocket exploded.

. . . Our cultural creation is founded wholly on a specific purpose. We do not conceive of a cultural and educational work unless it pursues some kind of definite, practical aim.

Ossip Brik,
From Pictures to Textile Prints, 1924.

German writer noted that the German poster makers took "the feminine type invented by Cheret, the graceful charm of which could only be destroyed by ruder German hands, and from this basis they created an ideal feminine figure, a kind of solid German Britannia or Germania . . . swinging a piece of soap, a torch, or a bottle of hair-oil in her uplifted right hand."[25] Cartoons portrayed these recognizable differences; one in *Simplicissimus* showed the ways different Europeans reacted to a railroad crash, relying on easy recognition of national stereotypes for its joke (Figure 5-30).

The focus on internationalism by early enthusiasts of commercial art had as its intention analysing and understanding national differences so that trade could take place more successfully.[26] Posters, along with all kinds of publicity, were seen as a reflection of national temperaments. America, in its attention to detail and all-pervading realism, showed itself a race "modern, materialistic, efficient and practical." The English, less practical and materialistic in outlook, expressed in posters the "sporty, stolid English temperament" of the open air. The Germans were seen by the same writer as imaginative and bold, typical of a Northern race. He contrasted this to the poster of France, where "the Latin temperament finds its expression in a lighter and more precious style—dainty, elegant, a little effeminate." Spain and Italy were gay and warm, Soviet Russia showed its agony in "constructionalism."[27]

These commonly held beliefs in national temperaments were on a collision course with the project of international harmony dreamed of both by political leaders and by advertising promoters like those in Carlu's Office of Graphic Propaganda for Peace or Frenzel's publication *Gebrauchsgraphik*. So closely was abstraction tied to internationalism that work like Malevich's and the architecture of Gropius formed the foundation of what later became known as the "International Style".[28]

Yet an attempt was made to find underlying similarities between nations. The deep instincts "which make the whole world kin" were sought: some located these in the area of feeling—laughter, tears, the love of the comic, the instinct of fear—more than in the rational.[29] Though the universal nature of abstract forms, line, shape, and color were mentioned by those commercial artists who were associated with fine arts circles, critics and clients of the poster did not delve so deeply into the sources of the artistic process. They considered the emotional qualities of the poster, the appeal to the passerby. Frenzel protested, perhaps intuitively feeling the danger in these nationalist stereotypes, and certainly seeing the threat to the international associations of advertising that he promoted. He argued that in spite of all national types there were "certain fundamental principles" that were the same for all people. These he called the qualities of the deepest and best humanity. As a proselytizer for advertising, he maintained that it was important to develop these fundamental, shared qualities for use in a "universal language of advertisement."[30]

In an early treatise on modernism, Kandinsky wrote that modern art ranged between two poles: that of great abstraction, and that of great realism.[31] Early abstraction was extremely important to graphic design. The significance of Russian Constructivism for design is that it was where fine arts theory and technique entered commercial art most directly. It entered pervasively and with great intensity. The radical culture of literary and artistic intellectuals—the circle of Rodchenko, Stepanova, the poet Mayakovsky, the writer Ossip Brik, the architect Alexei Gans and others—applied modernism to all forms of design and art.

A claim can be made for Rodchenko and Stepanova as the first graphic designers; here the profession of "Advertisement–Constructor" became conscious of itself. In France the abstraction of Cubism entered graphic design from Gleizes through Carlu, and with the Bauhaus and the *graphikers* it permeated both high and low design. The realistic, naturalistic art of the object endured, however, to emerge later as an alternative style for national purposes.

CHAPTER 6

The Funny Little Man In Propaganda and Politics

Whoever genuinely believes he knows how to save humanity from catastrophe has a job before him which is certainly not a part-time one.

PAINTER ROBERT MOTHERWELL AND ART CRITIC HAROLD ROSENBERG[1]

though the image of the FLM had been used for advertising (or commercial propaganda) and though idealists like Jean Carlu believed advertising could be "Propaganda for Peace," it was quite a different question whether the qualities that characterized this icon would transfer to propaganda in the service of politics. The opportunity came with the 1930s. But before graphic design was to be called on to sway political opinion, it would be applied to influence social habits.

Often used to promote alcohol and tobacco, the engaging FLM had represented these "vices" in the harmless guise of an infant. That they were not always considered harmless habits is seen by the propaganda campaigns mounted against them.

Poster Art and the Battle Against Alcohol

Most commercial artists were called on at some time in their careers to promote wines and beers. Zietara drew funny little men for Munich breweries, Cassandre improvised the episode of the Parisian boulevardier and his Dubonnet aperitif. The big beer and wine industry required plenty of publicity. Their needs were met, but there was a corresponding awareness of the other side, of the social costs of drinking. In France and Germany organiza-

6-1 *Hitler as a ridiculous little figure canceling the Treaty of Versailles, in a cartoon c. 1935.*

. . . Coupeau, conscious of Gervaise's anxious face opposite him, rose and declared that they weren't going to drink any more. They had killed twenty-five bottles—one and a half per person, counting the kids as grown-ups—and that was already more than enough.

Emile Zola,
L'Assommoir , 1877.

tions formed to publicize the evils of alcohol commissioned poster artists to get their message out. Such groups as the *Union de Francaises Contre l'Alcool* were active before the First World War. They solicited support through posters. To reach their audience—common people—poster artists turned to realistic illustration, scenes of domestic violence and public drunkeness. In such posters symbols such as the snake or the skull were associated with alcohol, and sometimes the realistic and the symbolic merged where a snake sidled from the bar to the cradle.

Pre-war posters commissioned by the leagues against drunkenness appeared in a society tolerant of alcohol use. To the French the evils of drink were associated with "hard" liquor, not with wines and beers, which were thought to be healthy and hygienic even for children. But in the medical profession there was concern about the large number of patients admitted to asylums because of alcoholism, an epidemic and a "national catastrophe." The posters aimed at reducing excessive drinking were realistic narratives, because it was the conviction of the medical experts that alcoholism was a "vice of the lower classes."[2] The French middle and upper classes believed that all workers were alcoholics, and the medical world concurred with pronounce-

6-2 *Poster by Bruno Gimpel of 1925 showing the effects of drinking: "This is what alcohol does."*

6-3 *Poster by Rene Ahrle, "Fight Against Alcohol," 1927.*

6-4 *Zietara's poster for punches, wines, and liquors sold by Diffenbach of Munich.*

ments that alcoholic excess was "less common among the affluent and educated."[3] Abstract art was no approach for this audience. Instead, they were shown the detailed representation of the home and its destruction by alcohol.

A tradition of anti-alcoholism existed also in Germany. Cartoonists in the satirical journal *Simplicissimus* ridiculed the heavy drinking of some Germans. There the serious problem of suicide resulting from alcoholism alarmed the medical profession, and artistic propaganda was enlisted. Here, too, the preferred style was realistic illustration and easy symbolism, like a worker being poured a glass by the skeleton of death. Bruno Gimpel, a prominent commercial artist, employed the contorted angles and wide staring eyes of Expressionism in the poster *So Wirkt Der Alkohol* (Figure 6-2). Rene Ahrle, a Berliner, used photography with cinematic, expressionist lighting to suggest the grimness of alcoholism (Figure 6-3).

But commercial interests promoted alcohol as part of a sophisticated life. When not accompanied by the convivial FLM, the bottle was offered by an upper-class charmer in full formal evening dress—top hat, tails, gloves, vest. A slew of formal FLMs appeared in the posters and pages of the 1920s and 30s, hoisting glasses together, redefining the bar as a meeting place rather than as the source of drunkenness. Zietara presented a perfect funny little man of the year 1930, dressed in white tie and tails, seated with his lady, advertising punch, wine, and liquors for a Munich client (Figure 6-4). The chubby, affectionate little guy once again takes the worry out of alcohol. Here he is with his round cheeks and shining eyes, a baby consumer of alcohol, conferring innocence on it.

The tuxedo-clad figure is a constant actor in the ads of this period. The crazy upper-class drunk, misbehaving, worked well in association with theaters and cabaret life, but not to sell products. He is often shown in posters acting out the wild times that could be enjoyed at those night spots.

The Cigarette Culture of the Twenties

More money was spent in the early thirties by the cigarette industry than by any other German industry except cosmetics.[4] The box for the cigarettes, the ads in the papers, the posters on the sidewalks, all were surfaces to be designed. To get away from the association of cigars with fat, corrupt businessmen, cigarettes were placed in the mouths of moderns, of girls with bobbed hair

6-5 *A modern woman of 1927, by Jobs Kuch, in a design for Summax.*

6-6 *Sketches of smokers by A. de Roux in L' Art Vivant, 1926.*

6-7 *Ad for men's tailoring, Berlin, 1928.*

Do you notice that strong cigarets make you shaky and do harm to your blood pressure? You might stop these effects by smoking NL right away . . . Smoking is healthy, makes you enjoy life, keeps you in good shape and you still have the calming effect of the cigaret . . . At your next purchase, require this excellent cigaret.

Nestor Lord cigarette ad 1928, translated from the German.

(Figure 6-5) and of elegant men.[5] The short hair provided a quickly recognizable symbol of modernism. To French readers of the sophisticated publication of the 1920s, *L'Art Vivant*, smoking cigarettes and briar pipes was part of being dashing (Figure 6-6).

The cigarette as a sign of modernity was held by slender, attenuated figures, sleek and streamlined like their cars. In both France and Germany, these figures became extremely slender (Figure 6-7). The sophisticated body in modernism was long and narrow. Identifying attributes of these upper-class fashionable figures became codified—the cigarette, the cigarette holder, the cane or walking stick, the spats. Occasionally an accompanying animal companion, hunting dog or deer, echoed Hohlwein and the aristocratic sport of the chase. Funny little men were of a lower class—even when they were dressed up they hung around the saloon.

When there was concern about the health hazards of smoking, the handsome slender man was the one chosen to pacify the viewer. In an advertising campaign for Nestor Lord cigarettes in the late 1920s, the handsome man advises worried smokers: "Smoking is healthy, makes you enjoy life, keeps you in good

. . . When you get closer to your 40s, worries, angriness, nervous disturbances, mental troubles shorten life . . . take your health into consideration while smoking, especially since you're aging. We're pleased to help you . . .

Nestor Lord cigarette ad in 1928, translated from the German.

shape." Worrying about being a "nicotinist" led one to change brands, not to stop smoking (Figure 6-8).

In the United States a cigarette culture connected with an urban, sophisticated life style inspired the design of many smoking accessories. Avant-garde artists in New York City designed asymmetrical ashtrays in geometric shapes that mirrored modern painting.[6]

The new Soviet Union encouraged smoking as much as the capitalists did, because the state owned the cigarette factories. The *"Klad,"* or *"treasure"* cigarette package, contained winning lottery tickets redeemable for a horse, a cow, or a tractor. *"Klad"* posters with text written by the playwright Mayakovsky showed workers, horses, cows, *everyone* smoking for the state. In other tobacco posters Soviet national types—workers, peasants, soldiers—sat on mounds of cigarettes and puffed hard for the state. (see also Figure 4-17)

National Types in Print

The outbreak of World War II was preceded by expressions of nationalism in the popular press. Countries were personified and recognizable. The satirical journal *Kladderadatsch,* still publishing in the 1930s, employed these representative figures successfully to communicate its political contempt for France, England, and Russia, and for the types of people inhabiting these countries. One cover (Figure 6-9) of 1936 adapts the old story of three men in a boat to make a political point. The boat is Europe; it's on the high seas, in danger. The strong man at the oars is Michael, personification of the German People. In front of him is The Frenchman (identified by headgear—a beret) who has abandoned his oar to pour a glass of wine. In the rear sits The Englishman, reading the *Times,* smoking his pipe. Michael is shown as muscular, clean cut, blond, neat, and forceful, the visual epitome of leadership. The Frenchman is piggish and negligent, the Englishman is aloof and silly. Only Michael can save this ship of states.

France's persona was the female figure, Marianne. She always wears the red Phrygian bonnet, a pointed cap with a cockade, the headgear of the French revolution.[7] In the pages of *Kladderadatsch,* Marianne appears in many forms—evidence of Germany's obsession with France bfore its invasion of that country in 1940. Marianne can be young or old, fat or thin, cross or cross-eyed, but most often she appears sexual and debauched. A

6-8 *Ad by Max Bittrof for Nestor & Lord, 1928.*

6-9 *Cover of the German magazine Kladderadatsch for April, 1936, showing the three men in a boat.*

6-10 *Cover of the German magazine Kladderadatsch for March, 1936, with Marianne of France embracing the treacherous Soviet soldier.*

sluttish Marianne with a cigarette dangling from her lips, her hair mussed, her clothing in disarray, reflects the German disapproval of French sexual "looseness." This promiscuity was equated with political infidelity. One drawing shows Marianne in bed with a Russian but dreaming of Franco of Spain. In others she holds a hammer and sickle. In a cover of 1936 (Figure 6-10) Marianne embraces the Russian soldier, only to be stabbed in the back by him.

Few representations conveyed as much loathing as those of the Soviet state. Germany feared the country to its east, the Bolshevik state. In this *Kladderadatsch* cover, the soldier is portrayed as Communists often were, with ugly features, thick lips, a scruffy mustache, and unkempt hair topped by a military cap with the Soviet red star. The patched uniform demonstrates that the poverty of the Soviet Union was known to the Germans.

Russians were often portrayed as ragged, bestial peasants, doing treacherous things, as here to Marianne. Only three years before the Hitler–Stalin pact of 1939, *Kladderadatsch* depicted Stalin as a murderer—Genghis Khan, Herod. Stalin's features lent themselves to caricature and easy recognition: bushy mustache, small eyes, coarse face. A peasant's tunic and a red star clinched the recognition.

The United States was personified either as the mythical Uncle Sam or in the figure of the actual president, Franklin Roosevelt. A cartoon from *Kladderadatsch* reveals the positive feelings many Germans had for the United States (which many regarded as a Germanic country); it depicts Roosevelt as Hercules slaughtering a many-headed hydra of enemies. Pictures of Americans in the illustrations of Joseph Leyendecker, Norman Rockwell, and others were reproduced in Europe in the 1930s. Leyendecker's figures, reminiscent of Hohlwein, showed preferred American types in advertising of the time: the well-proportioned figure, anatomically correct, presented as an ideal through the Hohlweinian heroic angle. Often a sports fan, the figure carries binoculars (a sign of the outdoors), leans on his stick, and looks over the field. Clean, correct, classy—those are the marks of the American ideal type of the time.

National types were not seen as a problem by analysts of publicity immediately before World War II. Differences in national character were unquestioned: the Germans were abstract and ordered, Americans young and healthy, the French had a genius for assimilation. But advertising showed that all used the same camera and the same soap, all drove cars and smoked cigarettes. It was advertising that acted as "the agent of human brotherhood." This supposed "unifying" nature of publicity led writers in *Gebrauchsgraphik* to continually exhort advertising artists to "fight in the forefront of the battle for peace."[8]

Dealing with Hitler in Print

An observer said of Hitler, "He was a very little man, but when he began to speak, he was blown up." At first artists, like everyone else, tried to dismiss Hitler, to minimize him through ridicule. This was easy to do—his appearance and his extremism were ridiculous. And Hitler's appearance lent itself to caricature. He sported two readily identifiable traits: a small black rectangle of a mustache, and a lock of dark hair plastered obliquely across his forehead. Many caricatures of Hitler appeared in the satirical

6-11 *Cover of the catalog for the exhibit "the Third Reich in Caricature," held in Prague, Czechoslovakia, 1934.*

6-12 *Cover of the German magazine* Kladderadatsch *for April, 1936, with Hitler rising in a balloon labeled "German Belief."*

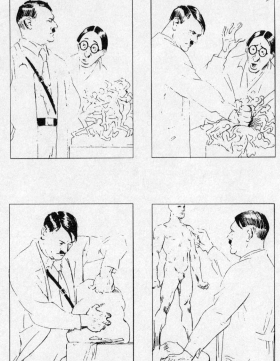

6-13 *A pro-Hitler drawing of Hitler in* Kladderadatsch, *titled, "Memorial to the Sculptors of Germany," by Oskar Garvens, 1933.*

journals and newspapers, in Germany and also in England, France, and the United States—so many that in 1934 an exhibit of them was held in a Prague gallery, though the German minister complained (Figure 6-11). The rising politician was shown in his underwear, as a bad child, as a fat beer drinker, a big balloon, a raging maniac, a circus performer, a cave man—any depiction in any style was sealed with the signs of the mustache and the hair.[9] His shape was distorted, his size minimized or inflated. The American publication *Vanity Fair* depicted Hitler in 1932 as an animated swastika. But cartoon and caricature did not hinder his political rise in the 1930s.

Although the opposition ridiculed him, supporters of Hitler represented him as a benevolent leader and the heir to Germany's ancient traditions. *Kladderadatsch* featured a peaceful Hitler holding branches of flowers, hailed by millions of German people or distributing gold to them (Figure 6-12). In conservative publications, including *Kladderadatsch,* Hitler is tall, realistically proportioned, quiet, calm, steady, upright and columnlike. Often he was seen from the heroic angle developed by Hohlwein, as though from below. In a narrative cartoon from 1933 (Figure 6-13), Hitler smashes the mess made by the "degenerate" modern sculptor, and recreates, with determined fists, a classical male nude. Hitler and the nude are both arrow-straight verticals.

Hitler and the Nazis claimed to represent the pagan Germanic past, admired as superior to the Christian period that it preceded. They used archaeology to validate these claims. Excavations finding "Germanic" relics justified invasions to reclaim the former "German" territory.[10] The symbol of the SS troops, the double lightning bolt, was adapted from an early pagan German sign, or rune. Hitler himself could be portrayed as an early Teuton or a shining knight of the Middle Ages.

Preferring idealized reality, Nazis favored illustration over photography. Illustration could make Goering leaner, and give Goebbels a chin. But designers of the 1920s and 1930s had discovered the power of the camera. In the invention of the political photomontage by John Heartfield, graphic design found its most effective medium for criticizing Hitler. Heartfield's new technique juxtaposed photographic images for bizarre effects. Heartfield cut, assembled, and pasted images from newspaper pages to make these montages; he also created them in the enlarger by multiple exposures. Many of Heartfield's creations appeared as covers in the workers illustrated paper *A–I–Z.*[11] Heartfield ridiculed through miniaturization when he cut Hitler down to size in his 1933 photomontage of the tiny Fuhrer watering a bomb-producing oak tree.

Memory of the violent antagonism between the Nazis and German Communists and Socialists in the early 1930s has been eclipsed by the larger disaster of World War II, but it explains many of Heartfield's most effective covers. A member of the Communist party, Heartfield opposed Hitler as a tool of the rich, the capitalist's collaborator, an oppressor of workers. In a brilliant photomontage he showed Adolf the Superman swallowing capitalist gold and spouting junk in posters seen all over Berlin in 1932, though Heartfield didn't escape until 1933, after Hitler took power. Another appeal to the leftist workers showed Goebbels advising Hitler to wear a Marx-like fake beard when addressing workers.

. . . When John Heartfield and I invented photomontage in my South End studio at five o'clock on a May morning in 1916, neither of us had any inkling of its great possibilities, nor of the thorny yet successful road it was to take. As so often happens in life, we had stumbled across a vein of gold without knowing it.

George Grosz to Erwin Piscator, 1928.

Nazi attributes lent themselves to Heartfield's photomontage. The swastika figured in many. Its circularity was brilliantly transformed into the medieval wheel of martyrs, the pupils of treacherous eyeballs, the sun rising over a Nazi swamp, or the cross of Christian Germany mutilated by barbarians. His most powerful montage must be the swastika's transformation into bloody hatchets in 1934.[12] Goering had personally restored decapitation as a form of execution, and that month four Communists had been beheaded with axes.

The Funny Little Man Comes Alive

Ridiculing Hitler in print reached a limited audience. For greater circulation the modern medium of the cinema was needed. And in 1940 a film appeared ridiculing the leader, or Der Phooey, of a country named Tomania. *The Great Dictator* was written, produced and directed by a funny little man who was real: Charles Chaplin.

Chaplin had created a film persona known as the Little Tramp, whose appearance in dozens of short, silent, comic films made him, after 1915, the most popular star in the film industry. He rocketed to worldwide fame—Europeans as well as Americans adored the "Charlie" figure Chaplin created. This figure came out of Chaplin's early years as an actor with traveling troupes of comedians in his native England (his actor parents put him on stage at the age of two). In 1913, when he began to make Keystone comedies, Chaplin added other original touches to his character.[13] Chaplin had perfected comic pantomime in England. When he started making American films, he remembers choosing "baggy pants, big shoes, a cane and a derby hat," and he added a mustache to make himself look older.[14] This figure of the "little tramp" became Chaplin's unique little man.

In many respects the little tramp is the FLM, animated. The figure, full view, occupies a movie set as a printed image lodges on the white paper. The figure is dressed entirely in black and white, and a sharp graphic effect is achieved from the severity of his costume. Charlie's black baggy pants, oversized shoes, tight jacket, and bowler hat form definite visual shapes, outlines, solids. The make-up of the face is the unnatural mask of the mime: an abstraction of a face, with painted, clown-white skin; heavy black eyes; lifted, exaggerated black eyebrows; and outlined lips. The mustache was a small black rectangle, consciously reduced in size so as not to obstruct his facial expressions. The

. . . Though a new note in comedy dramatics is sounded—in which the tragedies and heartbreaks of man's eternal struggle for happiness are made uproariously funny—there is, in addition, the Charlie Chaplin of old: the Chaplin of the little derby, the trick cane, the baggy trousers, the little mustache, sloppy shoes and waddling walk . . .

From the Press Book of 1925 for Chaplin's film "The Gold Rush."

high-contrast film stock used in the early years further increased the black and white artificiality of the face-mask.[15]

Chaplin's own physique contributed to the persona. His body was small (at a height of 5'4" Chaplin weighed 114 pounds), and he himself thought that it was out of proportion. He said "my head's too big for my body, my arms are too short for my body, and my hands are too small for my arms."[16] He played with those disproportions, exaggerating the size of the feet, pulling in the small jacket, enlarging the trousers. The mustache was obviously disproportionate, and the derby hat didn't fit his head but rested on top of it. The "Charlie" persona was a humorous misrepresentation of a human figure, something unreal, but accepted as a distortion that was funny.

This diminutive figure tumbled, tripped, and somersaulted on film. Chaplin's acrobatic skills, developed on the stage, contributed to the hilarity of his silent episodes. Charlie fell up and down stairs and escalators, slipped on rugs, tripped, skipped, and balanced precariously. In some ten-minute-long films, he fell two dozen times. Like the printed FLMs, he was unstable.

The movement of the Charlie persona was exaggerated by the slow cranking of the camera, which enhanced his "jerky" quality. This added to the artificial, invented quality of the persona. Chaplin's expressive body struck poses; in fact, some sections of his films appeared to be a series of arrested motion, attitudes connected by quick, mechanical steps: the "Charlie" walk.[17]

Chaplin evoked the admiration of moderns who worked in other media, who saw him as a genius of the new mechanical age, a creative artist like themselves, and a visual inspiration to them. By the 1920s he was internationally famous. In Paris the painter Fernand Leger made a drawing of "Charlot" (Figure 6-14). Leger fractured the figure of the little tramp and manipulated its elements. Starting with the components of the Chaplin creation, Leger abstracted them: the body is composed of planes of black and white, the cane is an arc and a line. The hands and feet are reduced to linear indications, the trunk is a bisected triangular solid, the bushy hair a geometric zig-zag.

The drawing was made a year before Leger's theoretical statement of 1923 on "The Aesthetics of the Machine," and the tendency to mechanical precision in Charlie's figure probably suggested him as a subject. Charlie is reconstructed by Leger as a geometrical abstraction, but he is recognizable from his gestures—the walk, the vertical lift of the derby hat from the head. Other painters in Dada and de Stijl also took inspiration from Chaplin.

6-14 *Fernand Leger's abstraction of Charlie Chaplin, 1922. © 1992 ARS, New York / ADAGP, Paris.*

6-15 *Constructivist cover of Russian film magazine Kino-fot 1922, the issue about Charlie Chaplin.*

6-16 *Photograph of Rodchenko and Stepanova with Kino-fot Chaplin cover in background, 1923.*

The same year as Leger's drawing, the Russian "First Working Group of Constructivists" devoted an issue of their new magazine *Kino-fot* to Chaplin (Figure 6-15). *Kino-fot* was published by Alexei Gans, the Constructivist architect and member of the Rodchenko-Stepanova circle. Articles by film directors and a manifesto by Rodchenko discussed Chaplin as an embodiment of the principles of Constructivism (Figure 6-16). His precision and his reduction to essentials were especially praised. He was hailed as a "constructivist" figure for his precise gestures and clean, mechanical movements. The little tramp was a perfect Constructivist visual metaphor—the geometric shape of his bowler hat, the line of his cane, the rectangle of his mustache, the planes of his black-suited body. His angular poses put constructivist principles into action. The issue of *Kino-fot* was accompanied by drawings by Varvara Stepanova, which condensed the essence of Charlot (Figure 6-17). At this moment the real man, Chaplin, merged with modernism's graphic invention, the Funny Little Man.

Charlie's persona seemed almost to have been created with the geometry of Constructivism. Stepanova's drawings stressed his circle of a head, topped by a semi-circle or an oval, the curve and line of the cane, the solid black or white played off against

6-17 *Three drawings of Chaplin's little tramp by Varvara Stepanova, 1922. © Estate of V. Stepanova/VAGA, New York 1993.*

6-18 *Drawing of Chaplin turning somersaults by Stepanova, 1922. © Estate of V. Stepanova/VAGA, New York 1993.*

the checks. Especially right was the way Chaplin arranged his body and props in a composition. No gestures were ever accidental, nothing was sloppy or unplanned—Chaplin's persona was an extremely controlled disportment of his own body and props in space. Isolated on a white page, the figure of Charlie became a graphic emblem of abstraction.

Stepanova analysed the piston-like quality of Charlie's movements (Figure 6-18). In "Charlie Turning Somersaults" she time-stopped his mechanical movements, the manner he had of bending one leg at right angles or extending his black trouser leg parallel to the ground. Chaplin used his legs in the way Jean Carlu depicted the newsboy of *Paris Soir*—they were abstracted into a straight line, with right-angled arms, hands, and feet.

Other Soviet artists embraced Chaplin. In 1922 El Lissitzky asked him to contribute to the periodical *Vesch*, along with Le Corbusier, van Doesburg, Cendrars, Leger, Mayakovsky, Severini, and others. As they exemplified modernism in other arts, Chaplin did so in the cinema. One principle of modernism was that the truth of the material itself should be shown: for example, concrete was not painted to look like marble. Chaplin used film as a new medium, with its own characteristics and possibilities, not as a substitute for painting or for theatrical drama;

6-19 *The Chaplin-Hitler figure merges in a cartoon, 1934.*

for that, they regarded him as an equal. Chaplin responded by expressing admiration for the new Soviet cinema:[18] his friendship with Russians and his genuine liking for them and their new Communist state caused him political difficulties in the later Cold War years.

In 1936 Chaplin began this most successful film, a piece of political propaganda. The resemblance between Adolf Hitler and the Little Tramp—particularly their little black mustaches—had already been noticed (Figure 6-19). By a strange coincidence Chaplin had been born within four days of Hitler's birth. Both were small, too. In a story of mistaken identity, Chaplin could play both parts. The idea appealed to him because he could speak for the first time on film, raging as Hitler while remaining nearly silent as himself.[19] The film, "The Great Dictator," ridiculed both Hitler and Mussolini. Through the added dimension of motion it was able to surpass what could be done statically in drawing or photography. One example of its effectiveness is the scene with the barber chairs, in which Hitler and Mussolini pumped themselves up to greater heights.

In 1940 Hitler invaded Poland, Belgium, and France; Chaplin released *The Great Dictator* in October of that year. It was a great success with the public, but its message of anti-Nazism was controversial since the United States was still offical-

. . . Alexander Korda had suggested I should do a Hitler story based on mistaken identity. Hitler had a moustache like the Tramp's so I could play both parts. Later it struck me that as Hitler I could harangue the crowds in jargon and as the Tramp I could remain more or less silent—ideal for my first sound film. The story took two years to develop . . . . Some of the vast crowd effects were achieved by putting Grapenuts on a tray above a vibrator! . . . As it was, I spent five hundred thousand dollars before I began turning the camera.

Charles Chaplin on "The Great Dictator."

ly neutral. It made problems for Chaplin, who had delivered pro-Russian speeches and addressed gatherings as "Dear Comrades."[20] A political film like *The Great Dictator* demonstrated the power of film as a propaganda medium. A recently established Senate Subcommittee on War Propaganda criticized such films as *That Hamilton Woman* (about Nelson and England's fight against Napoleon), *So Ends Our Night* (about European refugees) and *The Great Dictator*, citing them as documents that encouraged the United States to enter the European war. Chaplin was subpoenaed in 1941 to appear before the Committee and explain his motives in making the film.[21] The antagonism between those who advocated America's entry into the World War and those who put America First was resolved by the Japanese attack on Pearl Harbor on December 7, 1941, and Roosevelt's declaration of war the next day.

Advertising and graphic propaganda had proved a weak counterforce to organized force. New artistic techniques and new media were effective only when they were preaching to those already receptive. Neither hopeful efforts for peace by unions of graphic designers nor art by Carlu, Heartfield, or Chaplin delayed the war for a day. The universalism advocated by modernists was obliterated by national prejudices, powerful grudges, rivalries, and ambitions.

CHAPTER 7

Modernism Repulsed

*...Already the knowing brutes are aware that we
don't feel very securely at home within our
interpreted world....*

RAINER MARIA RILKE, FIRST DUINO ELEGY

7-1 *Poster for the Nazi Guard,
c. 1934.*

downward-slanting columns of type were the doleful symbol of Professor Frenzel's 1932 editorial on the state of commercial art, which he titled 'The Downward Curve.'[1] The intellectual and artistic level of advertising declined, as did hopes for a political and economic recovery in Germany. Indeed, while Frenzel facetiously wondered if all creative advertising artists had "gone to the North Pole," in reality many artists in Hitler's Germany were secretly wondering whether to emigrate, where to go, and when to leave.

Frenzel explained contemporary boring and trivial commercial art as being the result of economic crisis, which devalued talent as well as currency. As the publisher of international advertising and poster art, Frenzel knew the business world best, and interpreted the state of art in its terms. But he was prescient in observing that the current undervaluing of originality would have "evil results" in the future. Several of the earlier *gebrauchsgraphikers* worked on, but in a noticeably different vein. The funny little men began to disappear; in their stead appeared chaste architectural cityscapes or profile medallions of Goethe, like those on coins. Artist Oscar Berger believed that with "prosperity in the cellar" everyone needed distraction, and he advised that humorous touches like those he supplied with his little tip and tap men, could amuse the public. Other commercial artists with-

The city legislature should resolve that all funds authorized for any purposes of the Bauhaus, hence, including the salaries for teachers and employees, are to be canceled . . . The demolition of the Bauhaus is to be prepared . . . the funds becoming available are to be allocated for recipients of social welfare . . .

Minutes of the meetings of the City Council, Dessau, April 1, 1932, dissolving the Bauhaus at Dessau.

Dear Sir: I beg to inform you that the faculty of the Bauhaus at a meeting yesterday saw itself compelled, in view of the economic difficulties which have arisen from the shutdown of the Institute, to dissolve the Bauhaus Berlin.
Your obedient servant, Mies van der Rohe,

Letter to the Gestapo, July 20, 1933.

Our resolve was firm that the driveling Dadaist-Cubist and Futuristic "experience" mongers and "objectivity" mongers would never under any circumstances be allowed any part in our cultural rebirth . . . .

Adolf Hitler,
Reich Party Congress, 1935.

drew into a conservative shell in the increasingly inhospitable climate of National Socialist power. Even Zietara, who still tossed off an occasionally funny little figure for products, now found it prudent to take a serious architectural approach when designing a poster for a 1933 exhibition in Munich. Experimental modernists of the Bauhaus packed up and moved one more time after the city council evicted them from Dessau. Unlike the glorious architecture of Gropius's Dessau school, Mies van der Rohe directed the school in a warehouse in a suburb of Berlin. It was now a private academy of architecture, owned by Mies.

On coming to power in 1933 the new Nazi government issued a "German art report" outlining its attack on modernism. This report initiated a sustained campaign against modernism in the visual arts, including the rejection and denigration of all artists who had created its forms. It was a comprehensive attack, banning any building with a "boxlike" shape (Bauhaus architecture), firing museum directors who "wasted" money on modern art, and even forbidding the mention by name of any artist with "connections" to Bolshevism or Marxism.[2] Hostility to modern art was central to the National Socialist (Nazi) program. The Nazis consciously evoked a more glorious national past in art, when geniuses like Goethe, Schiller, and Beethoven represented German culture.[3] The present government could be legitimized, once it was seen as the successor to past periods of German greatness. So there were parades (literally and figuratively) of the pageant of the past, starting with early Germanic tribal warriors, priests, and seers; continuing with Gothic knights and the glory and crafts of the medieval period; trailed by the Renaissance, with its swordsmen and draftsmen—Durer, Altdorfer, Gutenberg—and on to a historical culmination in the SS, SA, Wehrmacht and other protectors of the Great German Art Exhibition of 1937. In an astounding medley of falcons, plumes, and motorized troops, the aesthetic and military were fused. One contemporary book, *Durer als Fuhrer (Durer as Leader)*, even proposed the artist as the great cultural–political unifier.[4]

Adherence to the glorious past (and to its styles and art) divided Germans. Those loyal to Germany, now led by the Nazi party, rejected un-German outsiders, those loyal to universal or international ideas. These could be identified and rejected by code words—cosmopolitan, Bolshevik. The ferocity with which the Nazis persecuted modern art is apparent in a leading Nazi theorist, Paul Schultze-Naumberg, who wrote in 1932 that the battle for art was a "life and death struggle," fundamental to the political goals of the Nazis.[5] Schultze-Naumberg put his words

Strictly confidential, State Secret Police, Berlin:
Ludwig Hilbersheimer and Vassily Kandinsky are no longer permitted to teach. Their places have to be taken by individuals who guarantee to support the principles of the National Socialist ideology . . . . The curriculum which has been in force up to now is not sufficient to satisfy the demands of the new State . . . a new curriculum accordingly modified is to be submitted to the Prussian Minister of Culture . . . . The members of the faculty have to complete and submit a questionnaire . . . .

Letter to Mies van der Rohe, July 21, 1933.

In the name of my fallen comrades I protest against the defamation of their goals and their works, for those which found their way into museums are today being desecrated . . . . These days pictures by both living and deceased modern painters are being systematically defamed! They have been branded alien, un-German, unworthy, and unnatural. The political motives ascribed to them are in most cases totally inappropriate. Artists are fundamentally unpolitical . . . for their kingdom is not of this world. It is always humanity with which they are concerned . . . .

Letter of Oskar Schlemmer to Prime Minister Goebbels, April 25, 1933.

into action by ordering that Oscar Schlemmer's murals in Weimar be destroyed. The attack on modernism culminated in the exhibits of "Degenerate Art," opening first in Munich (the art city) in August of 1937 to huge crowds, then traveling to other German cities.

The catalog of the exhibit "Degenerate Art" contained statements by the Fuhrer on the subject of art, testifying to his personal hostility to modernism. "Until National Socialism came to power, there existed in Germany a so-called modern art . . . . National Socialist Germany, however, means to have a *German* art once again."[6] In a most significant conflation of nationalism and naturalism, Hitler's Minister of Propaganda, Goebbels, ordered the confiscation of all works that either "insult German feeling, *or destroy or confuse natural form. . . .*"[7]

Such a directive allowed the massive seizure of paintings by 112 modern artists[8] in order to ridicule them in hastily constructed galleries. Paintings of abstracted or distorted figures, heads, and nudes were labeled as "this horror," "insult to German women," or "crazy at any price" (a Kandinsky). Paintings of distorted faces, including one of Oskar Schlemmer by his friend Otto Dix, were shown as "manifestations of degeneration."[9] Works by Klee and Kokoschka were paired with drawings by inmates in an insane asylum, and viewers asked to decide the better. What had been the formal experiments of Expressionism, Dada, Futurism, and Cubism were seen as the expressions of sick minds in the view of Nazi theorists. Prominent signs displayed the threatening words of Hitler from his speeches of the four years since he had taken power in 1933. Lumping together widely varying artists, from Franz Marc, a decorated soldier of the First World War, to George Grosz, a political leftist, the exhibit excoriated all avant-garde artists as insane, Bolsheviks, Jews, or, in general, "degenerate."

The theory of *Entartet,* or degeneracy and decadence, was based on earlier German pop–scientific books on race, which the National Socialists revived and dogmatized. The divisions of "degenerate" and "healthy" had appeared at the end of the nineteenth century. An 1892 book by Max Nordau, *Entartung (Degeneration),* attacked earlier art movements, and in 1903, Otto Weininger's *Sex and Character* described the inferior qualities of women compared to men, and found Jews and women to be prey to sexual passion, restlessness, and moral error.[10] It was the masculine Aryan figure of strength and beauty that symbolized the strength and nobility of the nation. The facial characteristics of the male ideal (Figure 7-2), representations of the nude

7-2 *Ideal Aryan male types drawn by Wolfgang Willrich, c. 1938.*

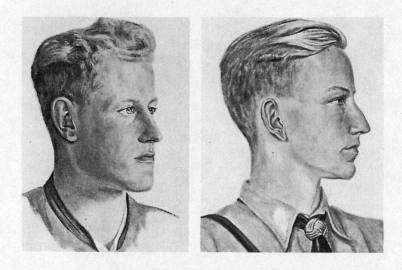

7-3 *Bronze statue of "Readiness" by Arno Becker.*

male, the male in action, all were at the center of the conception of the healthy nation-state. Another theorist of race, Wolfgang Willrich, published a pamphlet called "Cleansing of the Temple of Art." In it he took nudes by Nolde, Klee, Pechstein, Kirchner, and other moderns, and pasted them into collages that ridiculed the experimental distortions of Expressionism and other modern art movements.[11] These were clearly to be rejected as unacceptable versions of the human figure.

The FLM figure that we are following, unimportant in itself when compared to real human beings, was clearly a curious deviation from the ideal male figure, and fell (with no one's noticing it) on the outsider side of the line that separated the acceptable from the rejected.

Graphic Design Under Nazism

Critical to the identification of the "outsider" was the description of the "insider," the approved representations of the figure in art. The Nazis exhibited approved art in an exhibit across the street from the *Entartete Kunst* show. This was the *Grosse Deutsche Kunstausstellung,* or Great German Art Exhibition. A large sculpture by Nazi-approved sculptor Josef Thorak dominated the gallery; it was called *Kameradshaft* (Friendship) and showed two male nudes holding hands. Their exaggerated strength and size, their solid, straight-ahead look, their frontal, firmly planted feet, were meant to epitomize the power, the solid, unshakable will of

Aller Adel stammt vom Rosse

Dieses Sprichwort des deutschen Mittel=
alters knüpft an die ältesten Gedichte
und Lieder an, in denen das Schicksal
der Helden eines Volkes untrennbar
von dem ihrer Pferde dargestellt wird.
Mitgeteilt den edlen Reitern und Pferde=
züchtern, denen das Herz im Leibe lacht,
wenn sie einen ASBACH »URALT«
mit dem vollen runden Weinduft und
dem milden »weinigen« Geschmack
kredenzt bekommen.

7-4 *New style in advertising shown in Hermann Ahrens woodcut for wine, 1940.*

a nation looking ahead to a thousand-year Reich. There were other idealized male nudes, which were appreciated for their "realism" by the visitors (Figure 7-3).[12]

Commercial artists were affected by the new dogma. Throughout the Hitler period there remained a need for advertising, posters, book illustration, and other printed graphic design, and there the new Nazi policy on art appeared in its commercial dress. There was a great mining of the past. To express the spirit of wine in "accordance with the demands of the present day" the designer drew ornately costumed figures from the Gothic and Renaissance periods, equipping them with jeweled flagons and tankards to convey the "essence and origin of brandy." Knights in armor, heraldic devices, banners, horses, shields, prancing steeds aided this publicity campaign for alcohol (Figure 7-4). Former art schools opened as State Studios, led by sympathetic principals whose instructors in advertising, like legendary medieval maidens, relied heavily on knights in armor to win their battles. Hundreds of figures in historical costume accompanied products. With official encouragement, there was a revival of interest in peasant embroidery, antique hotel signs, and old Viennese shop decor. Endless numbers of illustrated books of fairy tales were published, located in the timeless past of Grimm.

The government encouraged traditional forms of design. The bookplate, for example, had fallen into disuse, owing to the "decline in the spirit of the German nation," but now, in the "stupendous rhythm" of the nation's recovery, this small cultural device was resurrected. So a competition was held to design a bookplate for the Libraries of the Reich Cultural Chamber, overseer of all the arts. The first prize united the devices of the German eagle and swastika with the Greek lyre (Figure 7-5).

7-5 *The first prize in the bookplate competition for the Musical Division of the Reich's Libraries.*

7-6 *Business ad by German graphic artist Herbert Barthelmaus, 1940.*

7-7 *New Year's Card in woodcut tradition, designed by graphic designer Albert Finistere for a client, 1939.*

Others used eagle's shields, and scrolls merged with the iron cross. The old closet full of attributes and symbols was unlocked and its contents used; past signs with meaningful associations were grafted onto contemporary projects.

Techniques as well as motifs of the past were revived. Woodcuts and wood engraving, long a part of the German tra-

Der Kampfbund für deutsche Kultur, Ortsgruppe
Frankfurt-M u. der Deutsche Buchdrucker-Verein
Frankfurt-M laden zum Besuch der Ausstellung

Die schöne
deutsche +
+ Schrift

im Kunstgewerbemuseum, Neue Mainzerstr. 49,
ergebenst ein. Von Montag, den 6. Oktober bis
Freitag, den 19. Oktober, von 10-2 Uhr geöffnet

7-8 *Invitation by the League of German Culture and the German Book Printers Society to an exhibition of beautiful German writing in Frankfurt.*

dition with such masters as Durer and Altdorfer to copy, were widely used in publicity and editorial illustrations. Herbert Bartholomaus advertised his graphic services—posters, trademarks, ads—via woodcuts in the old style (Figure 7-6), deemed "definitely German"; Abert Finsterer (Figure 7-7) did the same.

Typography in the early Third Reich could indicate political convictions. German type had been used before for patriotic purposes and it was now revived by the League for German Culture as the "beautiful German Script" (Figure 7-8). Gutenberg's black letter, oddly redefined as "picturesquely pictorial," had originated in a productive age, and the Nazis exhumed it to associate themselves with that period. On the other hand, sans serif type, like the Futura designed by the German Paul Renner in 1927, signified modernism. This modern typography was thought by the Nazis to be subversive, so much so that they dismissed Renner from his teaching position. His successor, Georg Trump, designed a black letter type in 1935.[13] Although no easy equation can be drawn between design and politics, it is fair to say that all the characteristics associated with Bauhaus modernist typography—asymmetry, sans serif faces, geometricized forms, rules and bars, abstraction (the search for "universals")—were offensive to the Nazis, and they punished the perpetrators. Such artists as Johannes Boehland and Emil Preetorius (an original member of the Munich group *Die Sechs*) mastered old scripts and hand-lettered beautiful posters during this period.

Nazi style was a motley mix. When the past evoked was Germanic, the preferred style was ornate; when Greece was evoked, it was classic. German artists produced landscapes, factory views, window displays, and pictures of fairy gardens. The technology of color photography co-existed with embroidery. The Reich was client as well as critic, and commissioned war posters and postage stamps commemorating the birthdays of Adolf Hitler, Bach, and Handel, and the plebiscite reuniting Austria with Germany. Stamps imitated Greek metopes with the nude male on a horse carrying the mail.

Under this onslaught of charioteers and knights, the FLM of the ebullient 20s was almost crushed. A remnant of his humor survived in the trademarks of Philipp Seitz (Figures 7-9 and 7-10), and even in a Funny Little Frau. The swastika made a head for one unique FLM (Figure 7-11). And the German Winter Relief Organization campaigned with a strange teapot-headed FLM to advocate meals cooked in one dish (Figure 7-12). Humor took a direction that can only be called corny. Figures associated with smoking were allowed to be humorous, if they were in period

7-9 *Trademark by Philipp Seitz, c. 1940.*

7-10 *Trademarks by Philipp Seitz, c. 1940.*

7-11 *Poster for German women's work, c. 1941.*

7-12 *Wartime ad for German Winter Relief promoting one-dish meals.*

7-13 *Tobacco ad in traditional costume and style, c. 1941.*

7-14 *Wartime ad for champagne, using cartoon cherubs.*

costume (Figure 7-13). And champagne was still associated with cheer, so alcoholic cherubs delighted Munich readers (Figure 7-14). But sophisticated design humor had emigrated.

Commercial artists had been specifically cautioned that art was not abstract but real. After Frenzel's death in 1937, articles in *Gebrauchsgraphik* warned commercial artists not to succumb to the movements of Impressionism, Expressionism, "radical" Cubism, and "revolutionary" Futurism.[14] Newly arrived theorists called abstraction superficial, evidence of a lack of ideas, a sign of no imagination. Artists who practiced it were "unsuccessful stylists" who could not see the absurdity of their work; they were tragic examples of aberration.[15] Qualities found in such capricious inventions as the FLM—liveliness, bounciness, instability—were exactly the opposite of the dignity, the quiet strength, the "restfulness" specifically pointed out as admirable in the figure. The pop-eyed little figures skittered off the scene.

Flight of the Moderns

What the Bauhaus preached in practice was the common citizenship of all forms of creative work, and their logical interdependence on one another in the modern world . . .

Walter Gropius,
Museum of Modern Art, 1938.

The official message got through to commercial artists in Europe. Many left. Jean Carlu remained in America in 1940 after France was invaded. Heartfield fled to Prague, then to London. George Grosz had accepted an invitation to teach at the Art Students League in New York. Lucian Bernhard had already opened a design studio in New York. Valentin Zietara had died of influenza in 1935. And the champion of "International Advertising Art" left, too: H. K. Frenzel died of a sudden illness that some friends thought might be suicide; certainly events had proved him totally wrong about the possibilities of world peace and understanding through *gebrauchsgraphik.* Of all the early graphikers, only Ludwig Hohlwein seemed at home in Hitler's Germany. Hohlwein didn't miss a brushstroke; the glorious chiseled beauties, poised as ever, modeled sport hats in one poster (Figure 7-15), while their clones in Nazi regalia modeled for the Reich in another (Figures 7-16 and 7-17).

Oscar Schlemmer seemed unable to accept the victory of totalitarianism over art. Prohibited from teaching, he remained in Germany and tried to support his family through sheep farming. Schlemmer had naively written to Prime Minister Goebbels in 1933, protesting the seizure of modern paintings. But both his paintings and a portrait of him had been included in the exhibit of Degenerate Art of 1937.[16] He realized, too late, that he should have left in 1933. But he lurched on, moving from place to place, suffering many humiliations—an exhibition closed, a job lost, rejected as "too old" for government competitions. He painted less and gamely worked at a paint factory testing lacquer, but in his diaries he recorded that this work depressed him.[17] From New York came word of the good reception given the Bauhaus show that Gropius put on at the Museum of Modern Art. Schlemmer was featured prominently in the show. Though he considered emigrating, Schlemmer never made it. The same day that Oskar Schlemmer died, Hitler and Mussolini met in Germany, and Rommel's army battled in Tunisia. Schlemmer's last entry in his diary was a quote from Rilke—a quote about art as the transformation of the world into pure glory.

. . . three Munich University students . . . were executed . . . for spreading anti-Nazi tracts . . . the victims were a medical student, Hans Scholl, veteran of Stalingrad, his sister Maria Scholl . . . a philosophy student, and another medical student Private Adrian Probst . . . they were guillotined after Gauleiter Gieseler of Munich had demanded that they be publicly hanged on the campus . . . the executions were carried out immediately after the sentence . . .

New York Times, Sunday, April 18, 1943.

7-15 *Poster by Ludwig Hohlwein, "The new Breiter Sport Hats," 1939.© 1992 ARS, New York / ADAGP, Paris.*

7-16 *Poster for Nazi party by Ludwig Hohlwein, c. 1939 © 1992 ARS, New York / ADAGP, Paris.*

Another Revolution

In the Soviet Union, as in Germany, the year 1932 signaled an ominous change of direction. Both totalitarian states considered art an activity to be employed for the government's purposes—art as an extension of politics. The revolutionary state had tolerated the revolutionary art movements and theories espoused by Rodchenko, Stepanova, Mayakovsky, and their circle, as well as other avant garde "isms," in the complex period after 1917. But in April 1932 a decree about the reconstruction of literary and artistic organizations dissolved all official art groups. The decree terminated the free, enthusiastic, experimental period, and foreshadowed the official doctrine of socialist realism that arrived after 1934.

. . . these [art] organizations might change from being an instrument for the maximum mobilization of Soviet writers and artists for the tasks of Socialist construction to being an instrument for cultivating elitist withdrawal and loss of contact with the political tasks of contemporaneity and with the important groups of writers and artists who sympathize with Socialist construction . . .

Central Committee of the All-Union Communist Party, Decree on the Reconstruction of Literary and Artistic Organizations, 1932.

7-17 *Poster by Ludwig Hohlwein for the Olympics of 1936.© 1992 ARS, New York / ADAGP, Paris.*

Varvara Stepanova, Chaplin's portrayer, survived as an active "production worker," a graphic designer of books, posters, and periodicals until her death in 1958. From both a practical and an ideological standpoint, printing in the Soviet state suited Stepanova. It was possible to get things done, because printing was one area of government production that functioned.[18] And official campaigns to increase literacy in the Soviet population meant that plenty of propaganda was required. Stepanova and her husband Rodchenko designed hundreds of books, posters, periodicals, and albums, and when she joined the only official union of artists she declared herself a book designer.

But the chill of the Soviet state's control of artistic production eventually caused Stepanova and many of her early idealistic

*On Rodchenko's photographs:
Why is the Pioneer girl shown
looking upwards? It is ideologi-
cally wrong. Pioneers and
Komsomolists should look forward.*

Member of an official Soviet jury, 1935.

*The basic features of decadent
bourgeois art are its falseness,
its belligerent anti-realism, its
hostility to objective knowledge
and to the truthful portrayal of
life . . . the reactionary tendency
in contemporary bourgeois art
is represented under the banner
of "originality." . . . Soviet
painters, sculptors, graphic
artists, the artists of the higher
social system called Socialism,
are creating a real people's art,
expressing the greatest ideas of
the present day—the ideas of
Lenin and Stalin—in the artistic images of socialist realism.*

Vladimir Kemenov,
Aspects of Two Cultures, 1947.

revolutionary colleagues to return to easel painting as the only way to fulfill their genuine independent artistic impulses. Rodchenko resumed painting in the late 30s. He continued to photograph, though with some official disapproval from the watchdog state. The end of his experimentation is evident in 1935. Rodchenko said, "I have stopped rebelling and trying to be original; I am no longer rash in shooting my photos; I no longer photograph in perspective for perspective's sake, nor from bird's eye view, whether it is necessary or not. I work on the contents, rather than on the appearance of the pictures."[19]

His flattened voice, unlike those of other revolutionaries, nevertheless survived until 1956. The poet Mayakovsky, vital center of early art movements, and early "Advertising-Constructor" of verses on cigarette and candy wrappers for the state, shot himself in 1930. Colleagues mourned this "energetic commander of the new revolutionary front of the arts."[20] Mayakovsky's personal depressions and failed love affairs made his "heart yearn for a bullet,"[21] but his suicide was hastened by violent disagreements with the Russian Association of Proletarian Writers, who wanted a literary return to the past of Tolstoy.[22] Mayakovsky's reputation was later restored by Stalin; but the poet's violent death puts a red stop to a period of artistic experimentation, destroyed by dogma.

The universe is asleep
its huge ear
star-infested
rests on a paw.

Vladimir Mayakovsky,
Cloud, 1914.

Captain

SO CTS.

AMERICAN CIGARETTES
MADE AS IN U.S.A

CHAPTER 8

The Funny Little Man Crosses the Ocean

The European is in our midst, either learning our ways and becoming like us...or not learning our ways...and turning his eyes back to the Europe that has disowned him....

MARGARET MEAD, AND KEEP YOUR POWDER DRY, 1942

the Funny Little Man emigrated from Europe with the Dubonnet liquor account; he landed in the United States in 1943. At first the American ambiance was receptive to this little invention. Later he was swamped, paradoxically, both by nationalism and by internationalism.

In 1943 printed images appeared in the many American newspapers and periodicals that brought the mass reading public news of the war, advice articles, popular fiction, and advertising. Periodicals had developed a special American look. The big four, *Century, Harper's, Scribner's,* and *McClure's,* had pioneered the use of illustration through wood engravings— *Century* had reached a huge public with its illustrated accounts of the history of the Civil War. With the invention of photoengraving it became easier to use illustrations, and their popularity encouraged publishers to add more pictures. Faster presses, the replacement of handset type by the Mergenthaler linotype machine, color printing, cheap paper, and other technology at the end of the nineteenth century caused an increase in the number of magazines. Scores of publications became the primary source of information and entertainment for Americans. Described as a "newspictures" periodical, in 1943 *Life* magazine reached nine million homes. Popular periodicals such as *The American Magazine, Collier's,* and the *Saturday Evening*

8-1 *Swiss poster for American style cigarettes, Herbert Leupin, 1946.*

. . . The second condition which gave the American novel its unique character was the naive Utopian theory on which the settlement of the new continent was originally based . . . Hence the American novelist was characteristically both a patriot and a dissident, and the failure to achieve the intended. . . goal could not be blamed on the English, but, as these writers recognized, was innate, owing to the facts of human nature. Hence a radical bitterness from loss of faith in man characterized the American novel from its early days and up to the present day, so that its prevailing and indeed inevitable style has always been ironic—ironic not only in tone but in essential structure . . . This American reader can feel in his Utopian bones the justice of that supposed "radical bitterness" generated by a background of unreal expectation, a bitterness to be felt behind the tortuous verbal churning of Faulkner as well as beneath Hemingway's surface of taut facticity—a naive, unending surprise and indignation that life is as it is. We cannot, unlike the Europeans, quite get over it . . .

John Updike,
Odd Jobs, 1991.

Post gave commercial artists the chance to make both editorial and advertising, images for the largest audience.[1]

Romanticized Realism

Illustrated images in the widely read magazines shared with descriptions in the text a quality that might be called "romanticized realism." American illustrators became expert in a style mastered by Joseph Leyendecker, and, later, by Norman Rockwell. One characteristic of this style was its complete and literal representation of its subjects. Perhaps the desire for completion expressed here has its roots as far back as the American primitive painter or limner. This untrained artist, a traveling portrait painter, doggedly included every detail—collar, cat, shoe—that gave recognizability to his subject. Since he had no academic training in anatomy, perspective, or color, he achieved authenticity by providing an inventory of personal, identifiable items. Later, more sophisticated and accomplished American painters like John Singleton Copley were realistic in a different manner—with training and genius they rendered the tactile reality of satin, pearls, and flesh, silver teapots on polished mahogany, as well as the puzzled eyes of Paul Revere and the double chins of Boston women.

But into the pragmatic representation of reality merged another strain, idealism, the motive for the founding of the Republic. This strain was refreshed by periodic rephrasings: "manifest destiny," "new birth of freedom," the "New Frontier," the "New Covenant." The reaffirmation of America as the desired ideal was a conviction not lessened over time but reinforced through waves of immigration. Hard work, ambition, and the Horatio Alger tradition sustained the belief in an improving world: things would be better tomorrow than today.

Portraits of this "real–ideal hybrid"[2] world filled the pages of popular magazines, companions to the romantic stories they also carried. By the third paragraph of any randomly chosen story, there was sure to be a rapt physical description of the perfect subjects: "The Lieutenant's incredibly blue eyes were disconsolate above his pink cheeks. He was the sort of kid who made good coast-artillery stuff—Culver, three years at Dartmouth, upstanding New Hampshire stock . . ."[3] Or: "The tall, light-haired young naval officer and the slender, black-haired girl who rushed breathless but laughing onto the Washington train were so handsome, so manifestly glad to be alive, that sentimen-

. . . *In the 1930s and the early
1940s New York artists were
able to assimilate and digest
Klee, Miro and the earlier
Kandinsky to an extent
unmatched elsewhere . . . none
of these three masters became a
serious influence in Paris until
after the war . . . . At the same
time Matisse's influence and
example were kept alive in New
York by Hans Hofmann and
Milton Avery . . . . In those
same years Picasso, Mondrian
and even Leger were very much
in the foreground in New York .
. . a generation of American
artists could start out fully
abreast—and perhaps even a
"little ahead" of their contemporaries elsewhere . . . .*

Clement Greenberg,
"American-type" Painting, 1955

tal fellow passengers thought. . ."[4] And the heroine " . . . Liz
looked like one of the prettier girls as she shrugged her head,
bright with feathery, soft red curls, up and out of the hood of her
rain cape."[5] These descriptions mirrored the ads promoting
Ipana toothpaste, Listerine mouthwash, Schenley's whiskey, and
the war effort. Illustrations were expertly drawn, anatomically
correct, faithfully colored. But in these four-color illustrations
there seemed almost to be another color on the presses: a roller
loaded with glow—an enhancing of the skin and hair and eyes
of these rosy, slender, mentally alert and spiritually wholesome
beings.

These legions of young and spirited creatures were considered typically American by European critics. Looking for national
types in popular commercial art, one critic wrote: "The
Americans with their preference for fine-looking young people,
fresh young girls, well-preserved elderly gentlemen, show their
loyalty to the ideal of a healthy life, in which gymnastic exercises
take up more room than philosophical speculation and comfort is
more important than pure esthetics."[6] The real–ideal permeated
the *Saturday Evening Post, American, Good Housekeeping,
Woman's Home Companion, Ladies' Home Journal* and other
mass media for the first half of the twentieth century. Its only real
competition was the cartoon, but that was limited to a few publications—the old *Life, Puck,* and *Judge.*

Illustrators Abroad

The merger of the common and the classical was deliberately
chosen. This version of the human figure was not the result of
ignorance or isolation, for by the 1920s American illustrators
were academically trained, often abroad. They studied at
Academie Julien and the Laurens and Colorossi schools of Paris
and Munich with Puvis de Chavannes or Benjamin Constant.
With no distinction drawn between fine and commercial art, it
was customary for a talented young American to study abroad.
Then, when he returned (few of them were women) he would
practice commercial illustration or easel painting, or both.
Illustrator Louis Loeb studied under Gerome in Paris, Max Klepper
spent four years in Munich. Jules Guerin of St. Louis exhibited at
the Paris Exposition of 1900, as did James Montgomery Flagg.
Others, including Glackens, Shinn, Hopper and Henri, became
better known for their painting although they did substantial
amounts of commercial work.

8-2 *Arrow Collar ad, J. C. Leyendecker, early 1920s. Courtesy of The Arrow Company.*

Awareness of the European tradition explains that the pre-ferred American image of the figure as it popularly developed was not a matter of provincialism, but rather that it was consciously chosen. In the academic tradition of anatomic detail, shading and modeling, tones and values, and athletic poses, America found its style. The extreme perfection of the academic statue was absorbed in class and projected onto the live models used by the popular illustrators on their return to America. On the printed page the ideal form from the Greek pediment drifted into American locales—the campus, the office, the train, the kitchen, the football field.

The real–ideal male figure appeared on hundreds of magazine covers, in fiction, and in advertising for men's suits, and socks, but most famously as the Arrow Collar man. This aristocratic figure, immaculately tailored, was seen from a point below eye level, the "heroic angle" of Hohlwein, to enhance his height and lofty status (Figure 8-2). This is not to say that there was any direct copying of Hohlwein. But the instinct to endow the figure with superior qualities was expressed in Leyendecker as in Hohlwein by a vantage point that signaled superiority. After all, for centuries human beings have looked up to the statue of the hero on horseback in the town square, or, more unluckily, up to the dictator on the balcony.

In Leyendecker the body was stable and vertical, or, when seated, gracefully relaxed—the arrested motion of the Greek statue. The lighting, aimed upward, exaggerated the planes of the noble bones and lit the hands that firmly grasped their modern props (cane, book, opera glasses). Noses unmatched since the Apollo Belvedere were looked down, and poses first seen on pediments surfaced at the opera. Though the deeply set eyes and carved lips came from Delphi, the coloring was usually fair—Germanic (Plate C-8). The creator of the Arrow Collar man and his like, and the perfector of this archetypal figure, was Joseph Leyendecker, who dominated the field for forty years.

Leyendecker had been the star at the Parisian art schools where he studied. Long after he left, teachers tacked his drawings on the wall as perfect examples of how to draw the body. In New York Leyendecker developed his style through thousands of commissions for advertising, magazine covers, illustrations, posters—all to support an elaborate mansion in New Rochelle, filled with antique French furniture and surrounded by sunken gardens and pools stocked with goldfish. Leyendecker was dapper in white flannels and blue blazer, straw hat and cane. He and his illustrator brother were short and dark, "like Spaniards" Norman Rockwell remembered, with delicate features and trim figures. Leyendecker was so sensitive that he dyed his smock to match the walls of his studio. He died in 1951, after falling under the "evil" spell of a man named Beach, a "huge, white, cold insect clinging to Joe's back" Rockwell said, who posed for the Arrow collar ads.[7] In the forty years when he was America's leading popular illustrator, Leyendecker lodged his Hohlwein-like idol in the American imagination. Every Wednesday the *Saturday Evening Post* entered three and one-half million American homes, every Friday *Collier's* entered another three million, and every month *The American Magazine* reached two and one-half million. In a country of 131,000,000 in 1943, this glorified ideal of the American male figure was pervasive.

What caused the American public to embrace such a classical figure? Perhaps the answer is to be found in persistent American traits. One was the "Utopian" aspect of the whole

American enterprise, the creation, out of the wilderness, of a country based on principles. Citizens of such a country could imagine a human being conforming to the "idea" of the human being, the Utopian being inhabiting the Republic. If the local bank was modeled on the Temple of Apollo, the banker could look like Apollo.

And their high level of craftsmanship helped the artists gain acceptance. Americans respected mastery of tools. The ability to portray the figure in difficult poses, drawing well, was admired. Since Copley, virtuoso renderings of surfaces—shiny satin, luscious peaches, furry squirrels, and highlights on flesh and hair and wood—elicited respect.

The illustrator was not always a graphic designer, but the American illustrators presented the products, alcohol and tobacco, that in France and Germany would be represented by a FLM. After Leyendecker lent his ideal man to Chesterfield cigarettes in 1918, the romanticized realistic figure advertised railroads, beer, grand pianos, whiskey, insurance, and felt hats—everything.[8] And the illustrator moved design into the fine art world, since it was close to portraiture and landscapes. The annual Art Directors Club exhibit was displayed at the Metropolitan Museum of Art in 1942, and one of the judges of that competition was a museum staff member. In 1949 the Jury for the Art Directors Show included three from the fine arts: two architectural historians from the Museum of Modern Art, Edgar Kaufmann and Monroe Wheeler, and the art historian Henry Russell Hitchcock. Graphic design was not well defined in the forties in America, with sliding borders between Advertising Art, Posters, Ornamental Design, Magazine Art, and a category called "Advertisement Design." The entire profession made tentative forays into fine art territory—the museums—for legitimacy.

The hyper-real figures sold products in America as the FLM sold products in Europe. The American public responded to a different icon. American readers pored over magazines and entered the narratives of fiction and advertising. They slid easily into the fictional body of the characters, so like their own but enhanced. *The American Magazine,* quintessentially a magazine of the people and the successor to a publication called *Frank Leslie's Illustrated Weekly*, had entered American households since 1876. The magazine knew its reader and in a house ad in November 1943 it issued this description:

> If you except the name. he is anybody's idea of the Average Man—typical looking, middle height, lives in a middle sized city, earns a medium income; married with

two children. He gets to the office the same time every morning, comes home at the same time, the same way, every night. He wears gray suits, blue neckties. Likes roast beef, and chocolate ice cream; baseball, mystery stories. His name, by the way is Kenilworth Endicott.

This "regular guy" is undistinguished in appearance; he is a real person (except for his name, which takes off on a flight of fancy.

Continuing with "Ken Endicott" is illuminating:

Ken Endicott has worked for the same firm thirteen years, been married to the same wife twelve. He has brought his income up from a junior clerk's to respectable tax brackets; bought a house, paid off part of the mortgage. His taxes and his insurance premiums are paid at once, his credit rating is tops. He is one of the people who has actually put a tenth of his income into War Bonds. He reads some worthwhile books occasionally . . . and *The American Magazine* regularly.

Here the typical male American is described. The type is industrious: he has worked his way up in the Horatio Alger tradition, and been loyal to the same employer. He embraces middle class respectability; wife, family, and home. He is thrifty. His patriotism, especially evident in wartime, is a long-standing national trait. Ken is successful, unpretentious, loyal, patriotic. Ken is an ordinary guy, who somehow belongs to the aristocracy of democrats. Ostensibly presented as ordinary, this portrait is actually of an ideal type, virtuous and complete. Ken is flawless.

The reader read the magazine in solitude, and entered alone into the fantasy story, or the narrative of the ad, or the article on "What the Boss Wants." The reader had a social relation with the magazine that was different from his or her relationship with the poster. The United States was not a big poster country. Although beautiful posters were made, they had never entered the culture of cities as they had in Europe, when Cassandre's first poster for *Au Bucheron* caused talk in the streets and angry articles in the art journals. The poster in the USA, the big billboard, belonged on the highway, where it was seen from a car traveling 50 miles an hour. Posters of the streets of Paris, the "art galleries of the people," did not work on Main Street. The European writer Walter Benjamin's concept of the street as the "interior" was foreign to Americans, as was the life of the *flaneur* who

Restraints and regulations imposed on beer and wine advertising have been a blessing in disguise. For they have resulted in the exploration of illustrative themes which might otherwise never have been born. Most effective, in this writer's opinion, are those campaigns which indelibly impress product identification on the mind and memory of the reader.
Examples: The Ballantine 3-ring cartoons; the Pabst Blue Ribbon Town characters; the Cresta Blanca girl with her purple-grape coiffure.

Annual of the Art Director's Club of New York, 1943.

8-3 *Magazine advertisement, "That Man is Here Again," Paul Rand, 1943. Courtesy of Paul Rand.*

8-4 *Paul Rand at Baruch College, 1986. Photo Al Cheruk for Artograph #6.*

idled along the arcades. Idling is *not* an American ideal. The life of the French cafe, where the Dubonnet man poured himself another as he watched the spectacle of the street, became, for Americans, the lonely cafes of Hopper, diners where "nighthawks" hung out.

Arrival of the FLM

The FLM tumbled into this American world as a salesman for the Schenley liquor account (Figure 8-3). The account included Dubonnet aperitifs, and it was held by the William Weintraub Agency in New York, whose art director was Paul Rand (Figure 8-4). In ads for *The New Yorker* and other publications in 1943, Rand used the same funny little man who had appeared in 1932 in Cassandre's poster sequence for Dubonnet. The wide recognition of the famous figure was evoked by the headline "That Man is Here Again," and Rand was hailed as the "artistic son" of Cassandre.[9]

The funny little man was received with delight; he was a change from photographs of liquor bottles, scenes of dignified gentlemen at their clubs, or pictures of gracious hosts at holiday parties. The old style was described as "antiquated, outlived and listless."[10] The FLM type, embodied in quintessential form as the Dubonnet man, began to appear in American print as it had in European. The peculiar merger of stylization and humor, and what was generally called abstraction, replaced for a while some naturalistic narratives on the American printed page.

In adapting this figure, (originated by Cassandre) for an American audience, Rand changed very little. He knew that the humor expressed in the little man was inseparable from the design itself, the manner in which the funny face was made, and the overall attitude of the figure.[11] Wherever he appeared, the funny little man had to "impart this same spirit without altering the original visual conception."[12] It was a spirit of conviviality. Rand added a printer's dot screen[13] over the head and played with the curves of the derby hat and the eyebrow—the Dubonnet man was all curves. In some instances he placed the little man in an environment, but it was the New England autumn, not a sidewalk cafe (Plate C-9). The basic figure, his body, his derby, his peculiar, identifying, doleful eye, was unaltered.

A second personification followed the American Dubonnet man. Rand invented a figure for the Coronet brandy account, a waiter whose head was in the shape of a brandy snifter. The

8-5 *Magazine advertisement for Coronet brandy, Paul Rand, 1946. Courtesy of Paul Rand.*

waiter carried a photographed bottle and glass in a bird's nest used as a tray. The effervescence of the soda mixer was suggested by the dot screen. A few lines suggested the face and hands, so that real and drawn objects appeared together. The substitution of the bird's nest for the tray said several things—springtime, newness, precious objects—juxtaposed against the flat shape of the waiter. In other Coronet ads, the process of collage allowed photographs of floating glasses on the effervescent screen (Figure 8-5). Rand's technique of collage allowed him to include objects in different media while keeping the impact of one unified composition.[14]

As a student of graphic design Rand had studied the work of European commercial designers in the journals *Gebrauschgraphik* and *Arts et Metiers Graphiques,* appreciating the work of Arpke, Deffke, Bernhard, Casssandre, Schleger, Zietara, Schulpig, Colin, Corty, and others whom he still credits.[15] At the age of seventeen he had lugged his portfolio, which was bigger than he was, to the Danish-born designer Gustav Jensen, asking to work for him because he admired his work (and his graceful signature) so much.[16] Instead Rand became an agency and magazine art director. He maintained such a consistent level of design inventiveness that by 1953 his ability was legendary.[17] Rand also studied Klee, Kandinsky, Picasso, and other modern painters, and he developed the skill to create expressive shapes and successful compositions.[18]

Designers and Humor

Rand, a playful aesthete, often used humor in visual design. For the Dunhill hat account he invented figures,[19] combining letter forms with stylized top hats, like a row of gentlemen at Ascot (Figure 8-6). In the experimental days of Soviet graphic design,

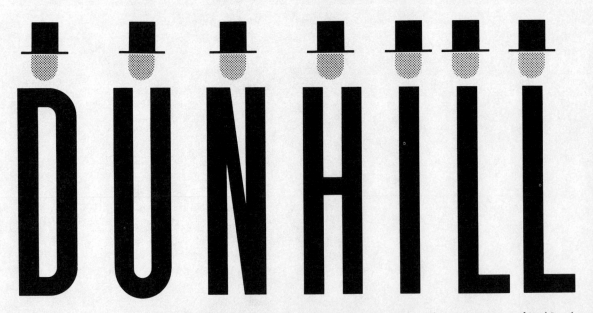

8-6 *Advertisement for Dunhill Clothiers, Paul Rand, 1947. Courtesy of Paul Rand.*

El Lissitsky had also created anthropomorphic forms out of the printer's job case. In a 1928 children's book he arranged and decorated letters to compose a story—a few lines for the hands, feet and head and skeletal forms of type (Figure 8-7). Adding such tools as the rake and hammer identified the types of the Soviet society—peasant, worker, soldier. Headgear made identification definite. Humor came from recognizing the figure and appreciating the similarity between the capital letter and the body.

Printed humor was not new, of course. In the pages of American magazines of this period there were many cartoons and caricatures. But unlike the Dubonnet man, where humor was an inherent part of the form, inseparable from the form, cartoons needed words, a caption, to complete the humor. In trademarks of the 1940's there were even some little men. One Mr. Nibbs represented maltless beverages, and so did a tuxedoed Mr. Newport. But these little figures were only abbreviated versions of a real figure. Before 1940 it was rare to find a successful abstracted, humorous, designed figure. Rand called attention to the use of humor in the serious artists of modernism—Picasso, Miro, Duchamp and others, seeing it as "a product of serious contemporary thought."[20]

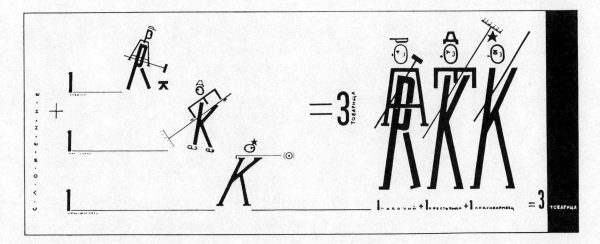

8-7 *Letterform figures from El Lissitsky's book for children, "Addition, Subtraction, Multiplication, Division," 1928. Here the page illustrates "1 worker + 1 peasant + 1 Red Army man = 3 comrades. © 1992 ARS, New York / ADAGP, Paris.*

Just as surrealism makes use of, or rather proceeds on the assumption of, the knowledge embodied in psycho-analysis, so abstract art makes use of, or proceeds on the basis of, the abstract concepts of physics and dynamics, geometry and mathematics. It is not necessary for the abstract artist to have a knowledge of these sciences . . . such concepts are part of our mental ambience, and the artist is precisely the individual who can make this ambience actual. He can make it actual in detached and nonutilitarian works of art; or he can make it actual in architecture and the industrial arts. In either case he is serving the highest interest of humanity . . . .

Herbert Read,
The Faculty of Abstraction, 1937.

In film, the FLM in the form of Chaplin's Tramp persona, evoked humor through his actions as well as through his appearance. Chaplin believed that humor always resulted from seeing someone placed in an undignified and embarrassing situation, and he invariably based his humorous situations on this principle.[21] The attribute he carried, the cane, became a part of the humor. Chaplin realized that to most people a cane identified a dandy. The Tramp's cane and his serious expression conveyed attempted dignity, which was undermined by his disastrous use of the cane—he tripped on it, he poked people with it. Similarly, the derby hat was essential to the persona of the Dubonnet man; something was lost when he appeared in a cowboy hat. For both Chaplin's Tramp and the Dubonnet man, the costume was essential to the figure.

How Designers Used Abstraction

Figures such as the Dubonnet man resulted from artistic techniques that transformed the object. An object was the starting point, but the intention was different: it was not to represent this object, but to take off from it to arrive at a new, invented form. The true proportions of the original object were exaggerated, distorted: a nose could be made bigger, an eye rounder, an eyebrow curvier. Parts could be eliminated. The object could be recognized with most of its parts missing, but the problem was which parts to keep and which to eliminate. Which were most recognizable? What attribute mattered most? Taking away the three-dimensionality of the object moved the work a step further away from representation. Areas of flat pattern and color, or of black, white and gray, replaced modeled forms. An underlying geometric relationship and linear or planar geometric shapes unified such designs.

Modernists, including Mondrian and Kandinsky, studied abstraction and published their views. In a more pragmatic way, commercial artists were apt to create art intuitively, then consider it intellectually, then revise it for the next assignment, in a continual process of refinement and understanding.

Dream, Displacement, and Design

Techniques in graphic design can be similar to those of dreams—focus on a central subject, exclusion of detail, lack of background, unreal surroundings. There is no real world with the constraint of real-world gravity, so forms can float and fall around. Disguising subjects and objects—the metaphor or the symbol—takes place. In graphic design this became the "visual pun" Rand wrote about. In a cover for a Museum of Modern Art book, *Modern Art in Your Life,* Rand substituted a palette for a dinner plate in a table setting. Instead of a plate, a palette. Like the verbal pun on palette–plate, the visual pun found the similarity between the circular shape of the palette and the circular shape of a dinner plate. For a 1941 poster for the same museum he replaced the beard of Uncle Sam with the sable bristles of the painter's brush; a few additional strokes made it a face. Rand wrote about this design process, illustrating how a dot could suggest a window, a button, an eye, a flower. Exaggeration, displacement, omission, substitution, fragmentation, and simplification—dream techniques known to designers.

Modern designers, inhabiting the world of Freud and Jung, sometimes intuitively expressed examples of the mind's processes on the printed page. Their use of geometry might be the conscious mind's attempt to impose a grid of order on the amorphous mental mess. Theorists of the modern, including Herbert Read, wrote of the concepts that were part of the "mental ambience," and named the artist as the individual who actualized this ambience.[22] Graphic designers who were also theorists, for example Rand, used and wrote about abstraction and metaphor.

In the streamlined modern world, identifying a type and signaling its personality quickly in print had to be done without attributes. Humor or congeniality had to emerge through distortion, through exaggeration, asymmetry, simplification, reduction, and all the other processes that modernism had made reputable.[23] The combination of all the artistic techniques cannot create inventive, amusing, memorable, or inspiring new forms; somehow it is the designer's unique talent that must put things together in a special way. Graphic design results from artistic techniques, but each design's special power is unique.

The Triumph of American Illustration

There seems to have been too long a history of a real-ideal tradition in American popular imagery for the FLM to convert the country to design abstraction. In 1942 and 1943, when the Dubonnet man appeared, mass circulation magazines were filled with true-life figures, most famously Norman Rockwell's. In 1941

Our task on this new Year's Day is three-fold: First, to press on with the massed forces of free humanity until the present assault upon civilization is completely crushed; second, so to organize relations among nations that forces of barbarism can never again break loose; third, to cooperate to the end that mankind may enjoy in peace and freedom the unprecedented blessings which Divine Providence through the progress of civilization has put within our reach . . . .

Franklin D. Roosevelt,
Washington, January 3, 1943

the *Saturday Evening Post* ran Rockwell's series of oil paintings, "Four Freedoms," which were based on President Roosevelt's remarks to Congress. Roosevelt predicted a world secure in four "essential human freedoms." These were "freedom of speech and expression . . . freedom of every person to worship God in his own way . . . freedom from want . . . freedom from fear . . . ." Rockwell's paintings appeared in the *Post* in 1943, in the middle of World War II, and they portrayed the kind of America the nation believed itself to be fighting for. The human figure was shown in situations that symbolized American values. The first freedom, Freedom of Speech, shows a plain weathered man standing at a town meeting, ready to speak. His companions, young and old, male and female, look up to him admiringly and listen to him. The second, Freedom of Worship, pictures people praying, their hands folded, heads bowed, shown in a tight close-up. The third, Freedom from Want, shows Mother bringing the Thanksgiving turkey in from the kitchen to the smiling family at the table, old and young, with Father presiding. The fourth, Freedom from Fear, is symbolized by Mother and Father together tucking the children into their bed at night; father's newspaper contains the words "bombing" and "horror" and a map.

In the paintings a bright light, like a flash, catches the subjects in a moment of action, frozen in a fraction of a second, and, like a flash, it catches every detail. It shows lines on everyone's faces, individual eyelashes, strands of hair, the shine of glass and silver, and loose threads on a worn jacket. The folded hands at prayer are perfectly distinct, working hands, with wrinkled skin and broken fingernails. Spatially some of the scenes are three-dimensional to the maximum, while in others the overlapping and compressed space resembles a telephoto lens picture. (Rockwell worked from photographs.) The close cropping of three paintings pretends to show a "slice of life," a moment when a spectator just happens to enter and catch a glimpse of a continuing situation. In this democratic baroque, one of the cropped faces turns to look into the spectator's eye, a device that Rockwell could have learned from Velasquez.

The hyper-realism of these paintings appealed to something fundamental in Americans, for Rockwell became America's most popular painter, succeeding Leyendecker. His desire to faithfully depict everything about his subject recalls the tradition of the early primitive American painters. Belt loops, spectacles, suspenders—everything is shown, and the desire for completion is fulfilled. The strict profile Rockwell often used is a traditional method of accurately portraying a person, long used on coins and medals. The imagination is not involved in the Freedom paintings. In fact, in case the messages are not getting through, printed words are included. The newspaper headline appears in the fourth, the title of the annual report in the first. Attributes identify the subjects—the doll for a girl, the apron for Mother. In Rockwell the combination of trained hands and primitive eyes resulted in an eerie literality, a super-real, which some called naiveté.

The Reassurance of Realism

Rockwell's realism gave American myths concrete shapes during wartime, when the nation was searching to define what separated it from the rest of the world. At one point the Council of International Relations initiated a program to develop a systematic understanding of America as a great contemporary culture, so that the new world, after victory, might be orchestrated to take advantage of each culture's special talents and values.[24] The anthropologist Margaret Mead was commissioned to analyse the American culture as she had the Samoan, to discover "with what qualities of our American character [we are] going to win the war."[25] Her conclusions, published in 1942, contemporary with the arrival of the FLM for Dubonnet, assumed that there was a special American character, its dynamics shaped by living through typical events in American culture.[26] Rockwell painted these events. He focused on plain folks, their progress from childhood, through adolescence and dating, to patriotic service, marriage and family life, and old age, all caught in humorous moments, "slices of life." Rockwell's prodigious output provided a fictional inventory of American types. Strung horizontally across the picture plane in a frieze—not figures swaying in a Greek procession, but perhaps a line of people waiting to vote, to see the doctor, to judge a cow—they acted the moments of American life. This calm disposition of figures across the picture plane ennobled each character in the illustration. It elevated them in importance, as much by each individual's command of space as by the careful rendering of their robes (or dungarees). The frozen moment endowed plain folks with a kind of stateliness—forever would this moment be remembered.

The family was the paradigmatic unit. In it there were the old folks, gray-haired and wise, the children, scrawny and innocent—boys troublemakers, girls good—the awkward adolescents. Young wives were usually pert, young husbands earnest.

Rockwell actualized figures in the community—the doctor, the mailman, the milkman, the barber, the druggist, the whole neighborhood. The anxiety and isolation that Mead found to be typical of Americans in the 1940s was perhaps allayed by the sight of this world of friends and friendly types. And the American ideal of community was satisfied by this fictional census, which established a kind of permanent village in what actually was a period of migration, uprootedness, role changes, and separations.

The American public appeared to be deeply content with the ever more literal and detailed renderings of their neighbors in magazine pages. This "reassuring realism" left little room on the American scene for capricious inventions like the FLM.

CHAPTER **9**

Goodbye Funny Little Man

*[They] have as it were their own inner life, know
their moment of maturation, and suffer debility and
ultimately a kind of natural death . . . .*[1]

FREDRIC JAMESON, MARXISM AND FORM

the serious business of war called for serious design. Such artists as Jean Carlu, who had settled in America, brought their style along and applied it to the American war effort. Carlu's pre-Pearl Harbor poster, the 1941 "Give 'em both Barrels," paired a war production worker holding a rivet gun with a soldier firing a machine gun. In his work for the United States Government, Carlu's previous inclinations toward propaganda for worthwhile causes materialized in dynamic propaganda. His huge poster promoting industry, "America's Answer, Production," influenced American public opinion in the critical period before the United States entered the war, when the political debate was between isolation and intervention.[2]

Carlu originally came to America intending to stay for two months. He remained for thirteen years. Apart from war propaganda, he worked on advertising campaigns, from Coca Cola to Sloan's liniment. But his later design changed, under the influence of Surrealism, and he tended toward a manner "less geometric, more supple and imaginary."[3] Always close to painters, Carlu knew the surrealists Andre Breton and Yves Tanguy in New York, and he incorporated some of their motifs in commercial art—disembodied hands, huge eyes, unusual juxtapositions. A greater change in style came about through his rejection of a geometric and "limited" composition, the kind he had applied in

9-1 *Poster by Hugo Laubi, Switzerland, 1940s.*

Paris Soir and analysed in his comparison for poster lovers in *Arts et Metiers Graphique* of 1928.

Carlu attempted to render sound into design in his 1949 poster for Perrier (Figure 9-2), where the clown listens to the fizz of the water through a huge enlarged ear. Carlu had been struck by the notion of making a "graphic symbol" for the fizzy water. By subordinating the brand name of the product to the slogan

9-3 *Poster for Perrier, "Pschitt," Jean Carlu, 1950. © 1992 ARS, New York / ADAGP, Paris.*

"The water which goes Fizz," the passerby, the much loved *passant* of his earlier analysis, must think "Perrier" when seeing the poster. Carlu believed that the effort to think of the brand name made it remain in the viewers' subconscious. He believed that he had been true to his theories, and the striking success of the poster vindicated him.

This 1949 poster possessed qualities that characterized many other renditions of the figure at this time and into the early 1950s. The change from his earlier tight, geometric structure led to loose, "unlimited" compositions. Carlu had previously used the "closed, rhythmic, geometric, simple" form and composition successfully.[4] But his later work had all the qualities he mentioned pejoratively in earlier years. In the Perrier poster the shape of the figure, a funny man, literally a clown, is unfinished, amorphous. The movement of the head, turning into a plane different from that of its ear and bottle, destroys the unified space. Instead of the flat angular shape of the *Paris Soir* newsboy, which formed a taut, contained form in one plane, the clown moves and looms and his form disintegrates. In place of pure geometry, there is distortion. Both early and late posters employ Cappiello's principle of a dark spot against a light background. But neither the distorted surrealist ear, nor the incoherent spatial relationship conform to his poster theory of the 1920s.

Perrier was followed by what Carlu called a less "percussive" poster, the 1950 "Pschitt Perrier" (Figure 9-3). This subject

9-4 *Illustration for magazine article with a debased FLM.*

9-5 *FLM form degeneration, in an ad for hair oil, late 1940s.*

9-6 *FLM form degeneration, in a comic strip ad for insurance, American magazine, late 1940s.*

has an even more amorphous shape, with its swooping arm reaching for the waiter. Its rough, sketchy lines, irrational composition, and illogical and contradictory draftsmanship contribute to the disintegration of its form.

The Dissolution of the FLM

Carlu's disproportionate figure prefigured hundreds of sketchy, amorphous little figures in American print of the late 1940s and 1950s. They indicate an overwhelming preference for the loose shape of the cartoon figure in place of the tight form of the design figure. Cartoon figures, little devitalized FLMs, illustrated articles (Figure 9-4), hair oil (Figure 9-5), insurance (Figure 9-6). Perhaps these little deformities are the result of the freedom to distort that modernism allowed, without the sense of design that talent provides. Expanding publications required more images, hastily drawn. The FLM may have become debased through overuse—so many clients, so many images needed, such urgent deadlines. Perhaps the possibilities in this form had been exhausted. Since the taut energy of early examples to the slackness of these later ones, the pliable FLM had appeared in thousands of variations.

The amorphous shapes of little cartoony men share characteristics with other amorphous shapes of the 1950s, the organic forms of Noguchi's table, of molded plywood furniture and the butterfly chair. Another key element in design, partner to the image, is type, and typefaces of the 1950s show a similar loose and casual appearance. Popular faces like Mistral(1953), or Dom Casual (1953), with their messy informality and irregular letters, contrast with the severe geometry of 1920s faces: Futura of 1927, Kabel of 1929, or Bernhard Gothic of 1929. As the circular form of a 1920s mirror epitomizes the purity of that geometrical style, a kidney-shaped swimming pool epitomizes the organic look of many of the drawn and designed forms of the 1950s.

In the post-war period, illustrators amply answered the needs of advertisers. There were humorous illustrations, fiction illustrations, product illustrations. There were straightforward cartoons with captions. There were caricatures, based on real people. There were line drawings, sketches, spot drawings. Everything could be handled by the talented army of illustrators in this period; no one style took care of everything.

Photography increasingly appeared in editorial pages and advertising. Alexey Brodovitch in Philadelphia and New York

The Revelations of Dr. Modesto

A Novel by Alan Harrington

9-7 *Book cover, for Alfred A. Knopf, Paul Rand, 1955. Courtesy of Paul Rand.*

advocated switching from painting to the newer, more modern medium of photography. Although Brodovitch himself had painted and designed in Paris, he advised his students to take up photography, since painting was dead.[5] Brodovitch was the art director of the fashion magazine *Harper's Bazaar* from 1935 to 1958, and its photographic pages established the standards of the period.

Graphic designers working in publishing, broadcasting and advertising used illustration or photography, but they largely ignored the FLM as a usable icon. Paul Rand used a figure on his book cover in 1955 that can be seen as the termination of the FLM (Figure 9-7). The figure is abstract; the humor lies in the visual pun of the substitution of the mirror for the head. But this elegant abstraction owes much more to the painting of Arp, modified by the subtlety of the designer's hand, than to the old funny men of Munich.

Goodbye to Chaplin

The animated FLM suffered a similar loss of popularity in the late 40s and 50s. Charles Chaplin, whose "Charlie" persona had been seen by moderns as a unique expressive form, was attacked by former admirers. Both his politics and his character were so reviled in those years that by 1953 Chaplin exiled himself permanently from the United States. In *The Great Dictator* Chaplin had made his statement against fascism. Like many socially conscious artists of that period, he had seen communism as preferable to Nazi fascism and he had been outspoken in his support of the Soviet Union. Like the Russian Constructivists, he had had a naive belief in the Soviet Union as a nation of equals. He had joined organizations calling for a second front in the war, along with such respectable statesmen as the Republican presidential candidate Wendell Willkie. But Chaplin was more deeply connected with the Soviet Union; he had made friends with many Russian moderns, among them Eisenstein, Shostakovich, Ehrenburg, and El Lissitsky.[6] In the course of advocating for aid to Russia, Chaplin had made imprudent remarks, which were widely reported in the press. Among them, "Communism happens to be what the Russians are fighting for . . . I am not a Communist, but I feel pretty pro-Communist."[7]

Chaplin's image as the lovable tramp was devastated by events in his personal life. A paternity suit was brought against him, and the FBI and other agencies invoked the Mann Act against him. (The Mann Act made it a Federal crime to pay to transport a person across state lines for sexual purposes.) Then the fifty-four-year-old Chaplin divorced his wife and married eighteen-year-old Oona O'Neill. The popular press reported the trials, including the lawyer's verbal attacks. (Chaplin was called a "Picadilly pimp" and "a little runt of a Svengali.") The fact that Chaplin had always refused to become an American citizen exacerbated the ill feeling against him; he was seen as a foreigner who had made millions in America—"a cheap Cockney cad"—who wouldn't become an American.[8]

In 1947 Chaplin exchanged the "Charlie" persona, silent, funny, and appealing, for the bitter murderous character of

Monsieur Verdoux. The film flopped. Professionally and personally Chaplin was rejected by the public.

Politically, support of the Soviet Union became unacceptable after Winston Churchill's 1946 Missouri speech in which he declared that "an iron curtain" had descended, which separated the free world from the Soviet. This began the period of the Cold War, and in that political climate the perception of Chaplin as alien, radical, and lewd, conclusively ended his viability as a funny little figure of innocent entertainment.

The Cold War and National Preferences

The economic prosperity during the war meant expansion, and that environment was as good for the visual arts as for everything else. By contrast, the Cold War seems a period of constriction. From Churchill's speech through the 1950s there was a climate of conformity, a suspicion of deviation, and a wariness of strangers. The trial of Alger Hiss, the rise of Mao in China, the Soviet Union's atomic bomb, and the activities of the House Un-American Activities committee strengthened these attitudes. The election of Eisenhower in 1952, with Nixon as his vice-president, typified the decade of the 50s; the soldier–statesman leading a peaceful, harmonious country, protecting its values. In general, a conservative and stable society.

Norman Rockwell continued to furnish the fictional documentation of that society.[9] A *Saturday Evening Post* cover in September 1954, entitled "Breaking Home Ties" (Figure 9-8), offers figures from the roster of American types. In this "slice of life" painting, a young man and his father sit on the running board of their old truck, waiting for the train that will take him to college. The young man is the agreed-upon American adolescent—alert, clean, tall, and gawky, red-headed, with big hands and big feet in new shoes. His Pop is weathered and downcast (losing Sonny), as he sits on his battered truck. The headgear of each is symbolic; Pop is holding both hats, a new white one for the boy, his own worn and broad-brimmed, matches tucked into the band. The boy looks down the track for the train, and his destination is telegraphed by the STATE U. sticker on his suitcase. He carries a wrapped package—lunch—and several books, partly read. While the boy is the central figure, the tallest and straightest, the father and the family dog are dejected, downbeat. Their lines are slack. The information is particular, literal, complete. The story is specific and without nuance. Further, this

9-8 *"Breaking Home Ties" by Norman Rockwell, on cover of Saturday Evening Post, September 25, 1954. Courtesy Thomas Rockwell.*

story shows one event that formed American character, as Mead suggested—in this case, leaving home. It embodies other valued American qualities in the plain folks of the rural scene. They've worked hard, they will sacrifice, they esteem education, they're unpretentious and honest.

In a telling coincidence, in the same month as "Breaking Home Ties" the *Saturday Evening Post* ran an editorial accusing Charles Chaplin of joining the Soviet enemy. Chaplin's friendship with Soviet artists, his pro-communist statements, his acceptance of a Kremlin peace prize, and other imprudent activities were cited.[10] This family magazine with its huge circulation echoed the violent press attacks on Chaplin that had gone on for decades. In the end his internationalism and nonconformity weighed heavily against him. Chaplin died in Switzerland in 1977.

The Disillusionment of the Moderns

The poster must not be seen as a unique work of art reproduced in numerous "examples," but conceived from its creation, in its essence, as an object in a series before being proofed thousands of times without variation.

Cassandre,
L'Art Vivant, 1926.

It now seems to me that I needn't be so afraid of seeming ridiculous if I were to tell you that I am dreadfully in love with Beauty and that it is from this unrequited love that I am dying . . . .

Cassandre,
letter to Lola Saalburg, 1950.

Nothing expresses the changed attitudes towards modern graphic design more clearly than two statements by Cassandre, one from 1929, the other from 1947. Cassandre had created the quintessential FLM in his1932 Dubonnet poster. Beginning with his first posters in 1923 he had been successful and admired, a proponent of modernism, a believer in the union of art and mechanization. Cassandre gave an artist's interpretation of art in the age of mechanical reproduction. The multiple reproduction of his poster was to him an advantage. Why? Because the poster would always be what the artist had finally decided it should be when he sent it to the printer. In preparing his designs for the printer, Cassandre used tools that approximated the texture of the printed sheet.[11] He sometimes used a stencil brush over flat tints of gouache in his maquettes to approximate the grain of the finished stone-lithographed poster. He supervised workers at the litho shop to ensure the exact translations of his work onto the stone. Sometimes eight or nine separate stones were necessary, and their combination and registration[12] could be difficult. Cassandre aimed to render the original design as the "one," and have it reproduced without alteration. Conceived with plumb line and rule, it used the tools of the engineer. The poster, thus "industrialized," was truthful. Cassandre's contemporary admirers believed that since the machine could not reproduce the soul of the artist, the intelligent artist—Cassandre—worked with the machine.[13] It was a kind of deity of our time, one who demanded sacrifices. To those who submitted to it, as Cassandre did, it granted perfect reproductions.[14]

In 1929 Cassandre openly adored the modern job of advertising, saying "publicity escapes judgment—it is like love—one does not judge love, one submits to it. It is a natural phenomenon like day or night . . . . One of the best and most beautiful consequences of contemporary activity."[15]

Through the 30s Cassandre enjoyed success in France and America. He designed for Brodovitch's *Harper's Bazaar*, and his posters were shown in a retrospective at the Museum of Modern Art in 1936.[16] But his own personality and unhappy events in his life contributed to Cassandre's mental depression. As the 30s

All my life, I have been solicited by two innate tendencies; a need for formal perfection, which has led me to pursue the work of a craftsman . . . and a burning thirst for a lyrical expression that aspires to free itself from all constraints . . . . But how is one to attain this joyful serenity when one's heart is filled with grief?

Cassandre,
papers, 1960.

Have I then forever lost the gift of feeling wonder, that sometimes frantic eagerness which set me on fire until I had completed what I was working on . . . .

Cassandre,
papers, 1962.

*I no longer want to go away
To grip the icy hands of the
      nearest shadows
I can no longer put off this
      look of despair. . .*

"Love Again," by Cassandre's friend Pierre Reverdy, translated by John Ashbery.[19]

But how can someone who is "madly" in love with Beauty and has experienced, if only for an instant, the dazzling light of Reality, suddenly start to love Darkness? . . .

Cassandre,
papers, 1962.

ended he wrote of his disillusionment, concluding that the poster did not have the power he once thought, to "break into the flux of days and society." On the contrary, publicity was "governed exclusively by special interests and that at all moments it interferes with the questions of propagating an idea." In a discouraged tone he said "art is always the dupe." Cassandre, who continued easel painting and theatrical work, said, "The reason why I have virtually abandoned advertising and now devote myself entirely to painting is that I felt nauseated by the perpetual confusion of values which is inevitable, given the present state of affairs."[17]

Cassandre bitterly rejected his optimistic convictions of the 20s, saying, "And so I renounce what I had believed for a time; that one can utilize the crude means of the poster to reach the viewer's innermost fiber, that one can reach him in his sensitive and emotional existence and awaken his intellect. That was no doubt asking too much."[18] Like so many other moderns, Cassandre had relished the new medium of art for publicity, for persuading, for improving and informing, for unifying nations and edifying populations. Like others, he came to realize that however powerful in theory the brush and pencil might be, they were easily broken by stronger forces. The fragile creator of the Dubonnet man killed himself in his Paris apartment in 1968.

The FLM Can Be Replaced

The appetite for humor once satisfied by the FLM was easily satisfied by other media. In the 1950s television sets became common in American homes. Comedy and situation comedy formed a large part of its programming. In time, the American desire for literal representation was pleased as network television provided "slices of life" by the dozens, with fictional portrayals of families of all kinds. These were peopled by the national types Rockwell had depicted. Homemaker moms, earnest dads, adorable tykes, benevolent grandparents, kindly community officials, neighbors, and fellow office workers filled the screen. Extended families and invented mixtures of parents, kids, adopted kids, step-families and other variations multiplied as TV dug in as the ubiquitous image-provider in American life.

These programs presented life situations as humorous, as Rockwell had. Though there could be conflicts, they were resolved through amusing actions. Central events in American life—marriage, romance and courtship, military service, adoles-

9-9 *Swiss poster for Capitol cigarettes, Hugo Laubi.*   **9-10** *Poster for the lottery, "Renversant," Andre Simon.*

cence, happy childhood, parenting and grandparenting—were seen as occasions for humor. This spectacle, these entertaining neighbors, alleviated loneliness in American lives. The magic of television cameras imagined any locale, city, country, apartment, house, or office, and provided a window onto its fictionalized life. Exact sets, real people, actual space, contemporary time, and natural movement satisfied the American thirst for verisimilitude. It was not necessary for a viewer to imagine, only to enjoy. The business sponsors of these situation comedies sustained the

9-11 *Poster for cakes in Lugano, by Franco Barberis.*

9-12 *European poster for paints, Savignac.*

realistic mood by using real people to present their products, adding to a world of visual literalness and "truth."

Some FLMs lived into the 60s in Europe. Casimir smoked Capitol cigarettes in Zurich (Figure 9-9); the lottery and the holiday cake were borne by other flying, frivolous Swiss FLMS (Figures 9-10 and 9-11). Italy and France still enjoyed them (Figure 9-12). The FLMS hadn't learned anything; they were still as precarious as earlier models, still perching, slipping, somersaulting, or turning everything upside down.

MATT GROENING

The Funny Little Man Redux: Is He Coming Back?

. . . And sometimes form, although it has become entirely void of meaning, will not only survive long after the death of its content, but will even unexpectedly and richly renew itself....

HENRI FOCILLON, THE LIFE OF FORMS IN ART

The history of art is like a vast mining enterprise, with innumerable shafts, most of them closed down long ago. Each artist works on in the dark, guided only by the tunnels and shafts of earlier work, following the vein and hoping for a bonanza, and fearing that the lode may play out tomorrow.

George Kubler,
The Shape of Time.

E-1 *Bart Simpson . The Simpsons© & ™ Twentieth Century Fox Film Corporation. Used with permission of Matt Groening.*

the 1980s saw a revival of styles and images thought dead since the 1950s. The FLM bounced back on the scene as a graphic salesman once again, this time for a giant American corporation. For a six-year period the "Charlie" persona of Chaplin was resuscitated to serve as the image for International Business Machines.

This corporation was known as a leading manufacturer of office machines, but when it came time to introduce its personal computer to compete with Apples and other computers, IBM needed a friendlier image than it possessed. The problem of designing print and television ads was given to the advertising agency Lord, Geller, Federico, Einstein.[1] The creative thinkers at that agency conceived of a large computer shrinking to friendly size, with a person reacting to it. A little guy, with whom everyone could identify. He would have to be in a black suit, to stand out against the white box. There was no need for him to speak—he was alone with the box—and so they thought of mime. Who else? Chaplin's "Charlie" became IBM's salesman.[2]

From the account given by the creators of the television commercials and the two dozen print ads that featured Charlie and the PC, it is clear that two aspects of the FLM, in its animated "Charlie" form, fit their needs. First, the personality of the little guy, hesitant but curious, resembled the potential customer. He is intimidated but eventually conquers the computer, just as the customer could do. He trips, makes mistakes, gets the door slammed in his face, but eventually overcomes the bigger opponent, just as Charlie used to do in his films. In a switch, the computer is miniaturized instead of the figure, becoming approachable.

The second element in the choice of Charlie was aesthetic. Charlie was chosen because he was a black-suited figure who contrasts nicely with the white box of the computer, the white Saarinen table and chair, the white vase. The technique of strong visual contrast, originally resulting from exaggerated make-up, crude film stock, and black costume, was transferred to television. The black focal image of Charlie moved on the white

E-2 IBM advertisement with Billy Scudder acting as Chaplin. © Bubbles, Inc. S. A. Courtesy of International Business Machines.

screen, just as the printed Charlie had lodged, a black spot on a white background of paper. The actor portraying Charlie, an experienced Chaplin impersonator, flies around, tilts on a chair, gestures, and poses. The camera was slowed to fifteen frames per second instead of the usual twenty-four to exaggerate his "jerky" actions. Charlie sniffs the red rose (which symbolized creativity to the producers); Chaplin often had used flowers with the Tramp. The music imitated scores from Chaplin flicks of the teens and twenties.[3]

The IBM/Chaplin merger was a great success. After the first commercial aired in September of 1981, more television ads were created, and over two dozen print ads, which won many awards. IBM was pleased. The campaign continued until 1987 (Figure E-2).

What the designers did was to leapfrog over the middle years of Chaplin's tainted image, back to the "classic" Chaplin, the little tramp everyone could still enjoy. The success of this selective revival with an entirely new public demonstrates the timeless appeal of the funny little persona. The graphic impact of the figure transferred to the new medium, print became television, the product sold.

This resurrection of the FLM once again called forth its opposite, the big powerful male, as it had in the past. In the late 80s American photographs for advertising revived the great Aryan 1930s masculine ideal. Figures for Calvin Klein Underwear showed the male torso, muscular, solid, unshakeable, in poses reminiscent of the work of the Nazi sculptors Josef Thorak and Arno Breker. It was Josef Thorak whose large male hand-holding nudes dominated the 1937 Munich Grosse Deutsche Kunstausstellung whose "Friendship" sculpture exemplified the worship of the male, his vigor and his bonding—strong men united—that was symbolic of the state and the German race.

The re-presentation of this Aryan model in advertising also appeared in Calvin Klein Sport ads. The male model bears an uncanny likeness to the drawings of physiognomies of ideal Aryans made by the Nazi art theorists Wolfgang Willrich and Oskar Just (Figures 7-2). The bone structure of the face, as well as the blond, light-eyed coloring, is an eerie replica of those sketches of ideal types. It had been Willrich who originally suggested to the Nazis their idea of an exhibition of "degenerate art."[4] The female ideal presented in the Just and Willrich sketches (Figure E-3) surfaced in perfume ads for Ralph Lauren at the same time as the Klein ads. Here the bone structure, with the heart-

E-3 *Wolfgang Willrich sketch of a female face, c. 1938.*

shaped face, small straight nose, rounded high forehead, delicate mouth, blond wisps of hair, and pale blue eyes match the 1936 German sketch to an unsettling degree.[5] Like Hohlwein's majestic creatures of the twenties, these ideals of perfection furnish a great looming alternate to the FLMs of their time. What dialectic requires that the small humorous figure evoke its opposite? It is unlikely that there could be any imitation of such an obscure source as the Willrich drawings, but what impulse from time to time asks for this ideal type as its expression?

Another Animated FLM

In January 1990 an electronic variation of the animated FLM appeared with phenomenal success. Fox Broadcasting introduced "The Simpsons," a half-hour television cartoon aired in prime time, which in three months ranked in the fifteen most popular shows. Characters in the show were the father, the mother, two daughters, and an irreverent son Bart, whose name is an anagram of "brat" (Figure E-1). All the characters deviate from the normal in their facial and bodily forms; the rubbery flexibility of the animation technique permits all their odd forms and unreal gestures. The genius of their creator, Matt Groening, makes all this distortion, anatomical impossibility, and unreal color acceptable. The Simpsons move in recognizable spaces, they live in real places—home, kitchen, school, nuclear plant—but they are weirdly unhuman.

The cartoon originated in an alternative culture and presents an alternative view of the domestic American situation, family life.[6] The program upsets all the stereotypes of the family. Parents are not wise, and children are not adorable but critical, as defiant as their parents are dopey. Community members are sleazy, and corrupt, businessmen are venal and hypocritical, and authority figures are wimps—pathetic. The inversion of all the former "family values" is what seems to delight the American public now. Critics propose that "The Simpsons" appeals to the working class viewer, the losers, who feel oppressed and abandoned.[7] This class, who can afford television but nothing more expensive, rejects the perfection of earlier domestic sitcoms. In the economic uncertainty of the 90s, contemporary critics say, they are just trying to keep going. They're not perfect. Theirs is the class that political parties court but television captures.[8]

The improbable Bart, center of family action, has the miniaturized, abbreviated, distorted shape of so many earlier FLMs, and, like them, he has gone on to become a manufacturing success. T-shirts with Bart quotes ("Underachiever and proud of it") sold at the rate of one million a day soon after the series began.[9] Beach towels, coffee mugs, decals, buttons, and bubble gum all sell—there are more than seventy licensed products. Bart also sells a popular candy bar. Bart is a simplified form, the body of a ten-year old reduced to its elements—truncated legs, blobs for hands and feet, pudgy middle, spiked head. Adding a voice to Bart, as well as the extravagant movement of an animated drawing, increases the complexity of his image. The figures of Bart and his family are produced through collective action. The complicated process of designing a narrative television cartoon involves the original creator, a team of fifty artists, and finally an assembly line of animators in Korea who add about 14,000 more images.[10]

It was appropriate for the revived and altered FLM to surface in television. Here is the replacement of the magazine and the poster, the combination of relaxation, information, and merchandising that those print media previously provided. In the electronic age, Americans get their information from television; seventy-five channels in some cities provide everything needed. A social factor contributes to the dominance of television. The streets, never much of a cultural locale, have become dangerous. Indoors is safer, and there is virtually nothing that cannot be seen via television. Fortress America, inside its protected homes, is linked electronically, as millions watch the same program at the same time, sharing exactly the same experience at the exact moment.

Aesthetically, Bart resembles the 1930 Italian Futurist toy of Fortunato Depero (Figure E-4). Certainly coincidentally, but in a strange confluence of style, the popular animated persona of Bart sports the same pointed top on the same abstracted body, the same aggressive, defiant stance projected by the angry doll of the Futurists.

This recurrent impulse to miniaturize the figure, to reduce it humorously (or at least not ominously) was a tendency some moderns recognized. But why this tendency? Putting the figure in a "doll-like" form, and enlivening it, makes it playful (not played with); it allows affection toward the figure. Oversize figures insist on the figure's greatness; perhaps they insist too much. The most thoughtful, expressive artist of modernism proposed that there had always been a tendency to a doll-like conception of the figure. Oskar Schlemmer asked if Indian, Egyptian, and Archaic Greek figures weren't "perilously close" to this image of human

E-4 *Futurist toy by Fortunato Depero.*

beings. It was the "doll, the reflection, the symbol" of humanity that emerged in periods of artistic struggle, he said,[11] suggesting a stage of simplification and abstraction toward "something better"—artistic truth. He advised his contemporaries to face what he called "bitter" evidence that the "way to style leads via the doll!"[12] The commercial funny man we have been following is a ludicrous little icon, but he has stubbornly held the ground until "something better" is invented.

C.1 *Poster by Valentin Zietara, "Bake With Yeast," 1921.*

C.2 *Poster by Valentin Zietara, for "The Six," 1914.*

C.3 *Book jacket by Thomas Theodor Heine, "Between Nine and Nine," 1919.*

c.4 *Poster by Ludwig Hohlwein for men's custom tailoring. © 1992 ARS, New York / ADAGP, Paris.*

C.5 *Poster by Jean Carlu for "Paris Soir" newspaper, 1928. © 1992 ARS, New York / ADAGP, Paris.*

c.6 *A. M. Cassandre's poster for Dubonnet, 1932. © 1992 ARS, New York / ADAGP, Paris.*

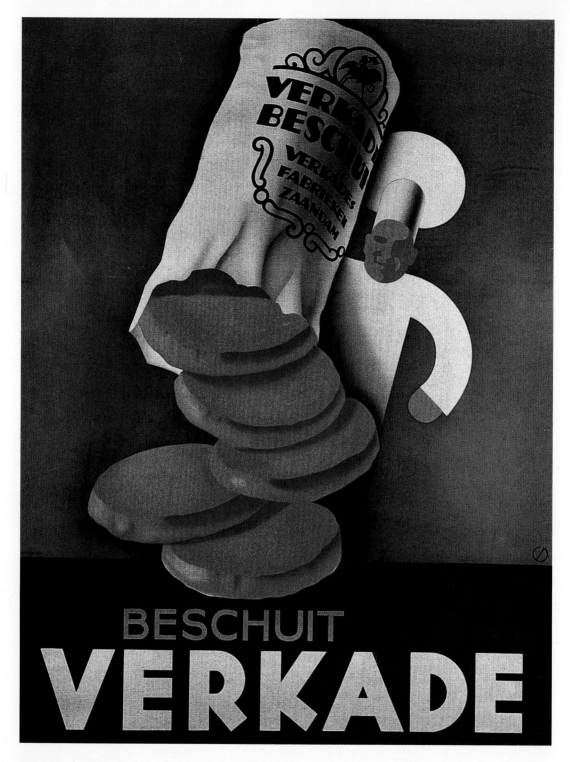

C.7 *Poster by C. Decker for cookies, Holland, c. 1936.*

C.8 *Arrow collar advertisement by J. C. Leyendecker, c. 1913. Courtesy of The Arrow Company.*

C.9 *Magazine advertisement by Paul Rand for the Dubonnet Corporation, 1943. Courtesy of Paul Rand.*

Afterword

making something smaller makes it childlike—then it is
harmless and cute. Insisting that a figure be smaller
can also be a way of insisting on its unimportance, of
lessening it. This motive appears in words—to "cut someone
down to size," or to "be-little" someone. The command is to "Be
little!" "Cute" is a short distance from "powerless"; "little" is close
to "lesser."

Graphic designers can consider whether it is something internal in the FLM form or something external in its environment that
determines the variations of such an icon, or even permits its survival. This FLM image suggested to some designers (for example,
Carlu and Rand) that form itself produces responses. Are curved
lines humorous? If so, other questions present themselves: When
done in what manner? When combined with what else? Only
when done a certain way? Only when opposed to other forms?
What technique has been applied to the standard human form to
make the FLM? Mostly it is miniaturization, and that should give
every renderer of the human figure something to think about
when altering proportions. Design students might inquire what it
is in proportion, in line or shape, what treatment of form, and
what relationships between parts that makes a design humorous
instead of abrasive.

Of the outside forces that affected the existence of the FLM, the strongest seemed to be political. Variations on this form, as with so many others, multiplied when no official approval or disapproval existed. During the Soviet Union's early promising years, Varvara Stepanova wrote of the "thousand creative possibilities" that lay ahead; there seemed no limit to the mysteries that free artistic exploration might uncover. The post-World War I period saw the momentous adventure of modernism and the experiment of the Bauhaus, along with light-hearted posters, art films, and a new conception of the designer. The spirit of building the future, the excitement, the openness that characterized early modernism occurred in free societies; political power, seeing art as its property, killed that trusting spirit of exploration.

The environment around the designer needs to be hospitable. If the designer is to invent, there has to be a climate that is not fearful of newness or of irreverence. Invention depends on the freedom to play, to invent without interference, to explore, to be one's own judge of what works and what doesn't.

Designers will continue to use the figure as an icon whose proportions can be manipulated and re-invented to express their meaning. They will study and use it as Goethe advised in a letter to a friend: "I hope you would contribute to working at a canon of male and female human shapes, to look for the irregularities that generate character . . . "[1]

APPENDIX *A*
A Scheme for Classifying the Funny Little Man

APPENDIX *B*
Glossary

APPENDIX *C*
Biographies

Bibliography

Endnotes

APPENDIX **A**

A Scheme for Classifying the Funny Little Man

This mutable graphic type appeared in hundreds of variations. It is essentially a miniaturization of the (masculine) human figure made humorous through distortion. It is a reduction of the full figure, exaggerating some elements, ignoring others, deviating from proportions accepted as normal. It is recognizable as a person, but it is not anatomically correct or realistic.

It is a controlled composition rather than a sketchy indication. The omissions come from deliberate elimination and abbre-

A-1 *Early type—simple miniaturization resulting in a dwarfed figure*

A-2 *Mature type—flat, formalized figure in motion*

A-3 *Abstract—a trademark*

viation, not from hasty rendition. It suggests, rather than details, form. It always was intended to be printed, reproduced mechanically, and therefore was a creation of professional graphic designers. It is two-dimensional.

It usually accompanied something else, something to be sold or promoted. It is not a cartoon, whose main purpose is to make a joke. It can represent a product, personify it, accompany it or stand alone.

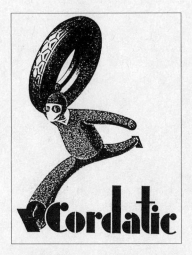

A-4 *Grotesk—animal-like or otherwise made to be bizarre*

A-5 *Caricaturized—based on a real person*

A-6 *Artistic—influenced by fine art theories and techniquesq*

APPENDIX **B**

Glossary

A few words seen in the art and text:
(G) German (F) French (R) Russian

Anziegen (G) Paid advertisement in a newspaper.
Briefkopf (G) Letterhead.
Buchaus Stattung (G) Layout of a book.
Canon The established rule, a set of principles to be closely followed.
Caricature A portrait of a person in either literature or art, which ridicules the subject by distorting the most noticeable characteristics or physical features.
Cartoon A drawing showing a humorous situation, usually in a publication. But it originally meant a full-size preparatory drawing for a fresco or painting, from the Italian *cartone,* a big sheet of paper.
Comic From the Greek *komos,* meaning to revel, to make merry.
Constructivism Modern Russian art movement after the Russian Revolution, most intense from 1918-1924.
Entwurf (G) A draft, a plan; most closely, a design.
Gebrauchsgraphik (G) Art for commerce. Frenzel defined it as "artistic means for the expression of a definite intention towards commercial propaganda." Utilitarian art.
Inserat (G) Advertisement.
Kalender (G) Calendar.
Kleingraphik (G) Graphic design for things smaller than posters—letterheads, trademarks, cards, and so on

Marken (G) Trademarks.

Metaphor Literally, from the Greek, carrying from one place to another. It is a figure of speech (or art) in which one thing is described in terms of another. A similarity of some nature is implied.

Packung (G) Packaging.

Plakat (G) Poster.

Porte d'harmonie (F) Literally, the harmonious door, or the "golden door." In French rural architecture, the relationship between the longest side of a building and its diagonal.

Prospekt (G) A pamphlet, a leaflet, or a brochure.

Publicité (F) Advertising.

Reklame (G) Advertising.

Schrift (G) Writing, handwriting, calligraphy.

Sachplakat (G) The "actual" poster associated with Bernhard and the poster designers of Northern Germany. The "real thing," so to speak.

Satire In Swift's definition, "a sort of glass wherein beholders do generally discover everybody's face but their own." Criticizing with wit.

Signete (G) a colophon—a printer or a publisher's mark.

Suprematism The Russian nonobjective art movement, after 1913, epitomized by Malevich's paintings of "White on White," c. 1918.

Traces regulateurs (F) The regulating lines of Corbusier's architecture.

Vkhutemas (R) Initials of the *Vysshie Khudozhestvenno–Tekhnicheskie Masterskie* (Higher Artistic Technical Studios) in Moscow. It combined in one institution the old Moscow College of Painting, Sculpture, and Architecture and the Stroganov School of Applied Art.

Werbekunst (G) Publicity art.

Biographies

Notes on some artists mentioned in the text, with dates when available.

Ahlers, Fritz. (1890–?) A self-taught artist, he exhibited in Berlin and Paris.

Ahrle, Rene. (1893–?) German, painter and commercial artist.

Altman, Natan. (1889–1970) Russian painter, author of "Futurism and Proletarian Art". Lived in Paris and returned to Russia in 1936.

Arpke, Otto. (1889–?) This "typical Berliner" designed posters, many for film; his most famous was for *The Cabinet of Dr. Caligari*.

Bayer, Herbert. (1900–1985) An Austrian typographer, painter, designer and photographer. He taught advertising, layout and typography at the Bauhaus in Dessau from 1925–28. He lived in America after 1938.

Bereny, Robert. (1887–?) Hungarian painter and commercial artist. Admired Cezanne; lived for years in Berlin. He was a member of the group "The Eight," who exhibited in Budapest.

Berger, Oskar. German painter and commercial artist noted for his humorous designs and his caricatures.

Bernhard, Lucian. (1883–1972) German designer of poster, typography, and other commercial art. He cofounded the magazine Das Plakat, which later became *Gebrauchsgraphik*. Moved to New York in 1923.

Cappiello, Leonetto. (1870–1942) He designed over 3,000

posters. His decorative drawings appeared in French publications around the turn of the century—*Le Rire, L'Assiette au Beurre, Le Figaro, Le Cri de Paris.* Theatrical posters were his specialty. The next generation—that of Carlu, Cassandre, and Colin—admired his work although they used a different style.

Carlu, Jean. (1900–) French designer of posters and book–covers, in 1932 he and Charles Peignot founded *l'Office de Propagande Graphique pour la Paix.* Lived in the United States from 1940; returned to France in 1945.

Cassandre, A. M. (1901–1968) The pseudonym of Adolphe Jean–Marie Mouron. French poster designer, painter and designer of sets for the theater and opera. Designer of typefaces *Bifur, Acier,* and *Peignot.*

Cheret, Jules. (1836–1932) A French painter and poster artist. An expert on lithography, he founded his own printing business, later the *Imprimerie Chaix.* He designed over a thousand posters.

Cissarz, Johann Vinzenz. (1873–1942) German painter, designer, decorator and interior designer. Taught book decoration and industrial design.

Colin, Paul. (1892-1985) French painter and poster designer, also a designer for the theater and the ballet. He opened his own art school in Paris.

Cooper, Austin. (1890–?) Canadian-born poster designer working in England.

Deffke, Wilhelm. (?–1950) In the early 1920s he was part of Wilhemwerk, a studio that produced trademarks for such German companies as Krupp and Pelikan.

Dix, Otto. (1891–1969) German painter in many media and commercial artist. Colleague of George Grosz in the "New Objectivity" or "Magical Realism" painting.

Drescher, Arno. (1882—?) German painter, designer of posters and designer of typefaces *Arabella* and *Energos.*

Erdt, Hans Rudi. (1883–1918) Berlin poster artist .

Fischer, Otto. (1870–1947) German painter of landscapes. Also an etcher and lithographer.

Frank, Hugo. (1892–?) A Berliner, designer and painter in watercolor, also a writer.

Frenzel, Hermann Karl. (1882-1937) Editor of *Gebrauchsgraphic.*

Gans, Alexei. (1893–1942) The principal theorist of Constructivism, his book *Konstruktivizm* was published in 1922. A typographer and graphic designer. May have been purged by Stalin.

Gimpel, Bruno. (1886–1943) German painter and commercial artist. Also designed stained-glass windows.

Ginsburg, Moisei. (1892–1946) Russian architect and professor at the Vkhutemas. He was a prolific writer, especially on public housing. His book *Housing* advocated constructivist principles.

Glass, Franz. (1886–?) German painter and industrial designer, member of the poster group *The Six* in Munich.

Gleizes, Albert. (1881–1953) French painter and leader of a group that met at Jacques Villon's studio at Puteaux, so known as the Puteaux group. They sponsored the *Section d'Or* exhibition of 1912.

Groening, Matt. (b. 1954.) American artist, creator of "The Simpsons", 1987.

Gropius, Walter. (1883–1969) German architect. First director of the Bauhaus from 1919 to 1926. Practiced in Berlin, then went to Harvard as head of the architecture department from 1937 to 1953.

Grosz, George. (1893–1959) Born Georg Gross. Discharged from the German army as unfit, joined Communist party with Heartfield, Herzfelde, and Piscator. Moved to the United States in 1932; 285 of his works were removed from German museums.

Heartfield, John. (1891–1968) Born in Berlin, he was originally named Helmut Herzfelde but anglicized his name at the outbreak of WWI to protest anti-Einglish sentiments. Fled Germany for England in 1938, returned in 1950, died in East Berlin.

Heine, Thomas Theodore. (1867–1948) German painter, illustrator and writer.

Heubner, Friedrich. (1886–?) A member of *The Six*, he designed landscapes and illustration.

Hohlwein, Ludwig. (1874–1949) Illustrator. designed posters, interiors, and books.

Horrmeyer, Ferdy. (1890–?) German painter and graphic artist who specialized in wall painting.

Kandinsky, Wassily. (1866–1944) A Russian, he painted his first abstract painting in 1911, was at the Bauhaus between 1922 and 1933, then moved to Paris. Major modern painter, writer, teacher.

Klinger, Julius. (1876–?) Viennese painter and poster designer. Worked with Koloman Moser. Known for witty posters, limited colors, simplification.

Le Corbusier. (1886–1965) The assumed name of Charles Edouard Jeanneret, one of the most influential architects of modernism. He was French, and he built everywhere.

Leger, Fernand. (1881–1955) A French painter, who wrote on the aesthetic of the machine. Active modernist thinker.

Leyendecker, J. C. (1874–1951) American illustrator.

Lissitsky, El (Lazar M. Lisitsky). (1890–1941) A friend of Malevich, he edited *Vesch/Gegenstand/Objet* with Ilya Ehrenburg. Taught interior design at the Vkhutemas. Invented *Prouns* (projects for the establishment of the new) 1919–1924, "a station on the way to constructing a new form."

Lunacharsky, Anatolii. (1874–1933) A Marxist activist who met Lenin and joined the Bolsheviks, he was the People's Commissar for Enlightenment from 1917 to 1929, during Constructivism's formation. He was tolerant of the avant–garde artists.

Maetzel, Dorothy. She and her husband Emil designed posters reproduced in *Gebrauchsgraphik* but little was written about them.

Mayakovsky, Vladimir. (1893–1930). Poet, artist, playwright *(Mystery–Bouffe)*, a founder and editor of *Lef*, central in radical literary artistic groups in Moscow. He visited America in 1925.

Moholy Nagy, Laszlo. (1895–1946) Hungarian painter and writer for *MA, de Stijl*. At the Bauhaus between 1923 and 1928, in Weimar and Dessau. Director of the New Bauhaus, Chicago, 1937–46.

Monkemeyer–Corty, Dora. She was mentioned in Frenzel's *Twenty-five-Years*, and her work was occasionally shown in the 1920s and 1930s.

Moos, Carl. (1878–?) Munich painter, designer of posters, lithographs, and woodcuts. Member of *The Six*.

Mouron, Alphonse. (see Cassandre.)

Nitsche, Erich. (1908–?) Swiss–American advertising artist and poster designer.

Nitsche, Julius. Poster artist in Munich around 1915.

Popova, Liubov. (1889–1924) Constructivist stage designer, and textile designer. Professor at the Vkhutemas .

Preetorius, Emil. Member of *The Six*.

Rand, Paul. (b.1914.) American designer, writer, and teacher.

Rockwell, Norman. (1894–1978) American illustrator; many *Saturday Evening Post* covers.

Rodchenko, Alexander. (1891–1956) A leader of the Russian Constructivists, teacher at the Vkhutemas, designer, painter, sculptor, photographer, husband of Varvara Stepanova.

Schauroth, Lina von. An artist working in the style of Bernhard, she did patriotic posters during World War I.

Schlemmer, Oskar. (1888–1943) German painter, actor, teacher at the Bauhaus in Weimar and Dessau from 1920 to 1929; maker of theater, murals, and theory.

Schulpig, Karl. (1884–1948) German painter and commercial artist specializing in trademarks. Known also for wood engravings.

Schwarzer, Max. A member of *The Six*, he practiced around 1914.

Steiner, Joseph. (1882–?) Swiss architect and industrial designer.

Steiner, Julius. (1878 –?) Born in Budapest, he was a graphic artist in Berlin.

Stepanova, Varvara. (1894–1958) Artist in many media; book designer, stage designer *(Death of Tarelkin)*, closely associated with *Lef, Novyi Lef,* and the theoretical formulation of Constructivism. Married to Rodchenko.

Thorak, Josef. (1889–1952) Austrian sculptor. Created many massive monuments and enjoyed great popularity during the Nazi period; afterward he was ostracized and most of his works were destroyed.

Vesnin, Alexander. (1883–1959) Architect and president of the Constructivist architectural group, the Union of Contemporary Architects. Editor with Moisei Ginsburg of the journal *CA.* A professor at the Vkhutemas.

Virl, Hermann. (1903–1958) German painter and commercial artist, who headed a printing school in the Nazi period.

Willrich, Wolfgang. (1897–?) German painter of figures and writer of racist tracts. Prominent in the formation of the "Degenerate Art" exhibit.

Zietara, Valentin. (1883–1935). Born in Poland, he lived in Munich and was influential in forming the Munich style poster. He was a member of *The Six*.

Data has been derived from Vollmer, Theime–Becker, Benezit, Chipp, Hamilton, Bowlt, Meggs, and Weill. Dates for some artists are not available.

Bibliography

The Funny LIttle Man by Virginia Smith

Periodicals

German

Das Plakat 1910–21
Gebrauchsgraphik 1925–41
Kladderadatsch
Simplicissimus

French

Arts et Metiers Graphiques
L'Art Internationale
*   d'aujourd'hui*
L'Art Vivant
L'Esprit Nouveau

Russian
Lef (Left Front of the Arts)

American

Art Directors Club Annual
Esquire
Redbook
Saturday Evening Post
The American Magazine
The New York Times

Other

Graphis
Graphis Annual

Reference

Benezit, Emmanuel. 1976. *Dictionnaire critique et documentaire des Peintres, Sculpteurs, Dessinateurs et Graveurs.* 10 vols. Paris: Librairie Grund.

Bowlt, John E., Editor and translator. 1976. *Russian Art of the Avant–Garde: Theory and Criticism 1902–1934.* New York: Viking.

Chipp, Herschel. 1968. *Theories of Modern Art: A Source Book by Artists and Critics.* Berkeley and Los Angeles: University of California Press.

Fawcett, Trevor, and Clive Phillpot. 1976. *The Art Press.* London: Art Book Co.

Hamilton, George Heard. 1983. *Painting and Sculpture in Europe, 1880–1940.* England: Penguin Books.

Meggs, Philip. 1983. *A History of Graphic Design.* New York: Van Nostrand Reinhold.

Mott, Frank Luther. 1968. *A History of American Magazines.* 5 vols. Cambridge, MA: The Belknap Press of Harvard University Press.

Popitz, Klaus, et al. 1980. *Das Fruhe Plakat In Europa und den USA.* 3 vols. Berlin: Mann.

Thieme–Becker. 1907–50. *Allgemeines Lexikon Der Bildenden Kunstler.* 37 vols. Leipsig: Engelman.

Vollmer, Hans. 1953–62. *Allgemeines Lexicon Der Bildenden Kunstler.* 6 vols. Leipsig: Seeman.

Wingler, Hans. 1969. *The Bauhaus.* Cambridge, MA: The MIT Press. Originally *Das Bauhaus,* Cologne, 1962.

General

Allen, Ann Taylor. 1984. *Satire and Society In Wilhelmine Germany 1890–1914.* Lexington: University Press of Kentucky.

Barron, Stephanie. 1991. *"Degenerate Art": The Fate of the Avant Garde in Nazi Germany.* New York: Harry N. Abrams.

Bayer, Herbert, editor, with Walter Gropius and Ise Gropius. 1938. *Bauhaus 1919–1928.* New York: The Museum of Modern Art.

Benjamin, Walter. 1973. *Charles Baudelaire: A Lyric Poet in the Era of High Capitalism.* London: NLB.

Bowie, Theodore, editor, 1959. *The Sketchbook of Villard de Honnecourt.* 2nd edition, revised. Bloomington: Indiana

University. Distributed by George Wittenborn, Inc., New York.

Brown, Edward. 1973. *Mayakovsky: A Poet in the Revolution.* Princeton, NJ: Princeton University Press.

Carlu, Jean. "Reflexions sur L'Esthetique de L'Affiche." *Arts et Metiers Graphiques,* 1928–29.

Cassandre, A. M. 1933. "Art and Poster Art." *Gebrauchsgraphik #1.*

———. 1929. "Publicite," *l' Art Internationale d'aujourd'hui #12.* Paris: Moreau.

Chaplin, Charles. 1975. *My Life in Pictures.* New York: Grosset & Dunlap.

Chefdor, Monique. 1980. *Blaise Cendrars.* Boston: Twayne Publishers.

Chernevich, Elena, and Mikhail Anikst. 1987. *Soviet Commercial Design of the Twenties.* New York: Abbeville.

Cheronnet, Louis. 1926. "La Publicite Moderne: Fernand Leger and Robert Delaunay." *L'Art Vivant.* Paris: Librairie Larousse.

Crawford, W. S. 1925. "The Poster." *Gebrauchsgraphik #5.*

Dupuy, Roger–Louis. 1932. "French Commercial Art." *Gebrauchsgraphik #6.*

———. 1929. "Jean Carlu, A French Poster Artist." *Gebrauchsgraphik , #6.*

———. 1926. "L'Affiche Francaise." *Gebrauchsgraphik #7.*

Eagleton, Terry. 1981. *Walter Benjamin, or Towards a revolutionary criticism.* London: Verso Editions and NLB.

Elliott, David, editor, 1979. *Rodchenko and The Arts of Revolutionary Russia.* NY: Pantheon.

Frenzel, H. K. 1931. "Brief Remarks on Pictorial Form in Advertising," *Gebrauchsgraphik #5.*

———. 1926a. "The Foreign Poster." *Gebrauchsgraphik #3.*

———. 1926b. *Ludwig Hohlwein.* Berlin: Phonix Illustrations.

———. 1925a. "25 Years of German Poster. "*Gebrauchsgraphik #4.*

———. 1925b. "Zietara: Das Originelle Plakat." *Gebrauchsgraphik #6.*

Frisby, David. 1986. *Fragments of Modernity.* Cambridge, MA: The MIT Press.

Gay, Peter. 1968. Weimar Culture. New York: Harper & Row.

Gray, Camilla. 1962. *The Russian Experiment in Art 1863-1922.* Revised by Marian Burleigh-Motley, 1986. London: Thames & Hudson.

Gropius, Walter. 1961. *Theater of the Bauhaus.* Middletown: Wesleyan University Press.

Halina, Stephan. 1981. *"Lef" and the Left Front of the Arts.* Munich: Otto Sagner.

Heller, Erich. 1972. *The Disinherited Mind: Essays in Modern German Literature and Thought.* London: Bowes & Bowes.

Heller, Steven. 1979. "The Late, Great Simplicissimus." *Print,* September–October, pp. 33–43.

Hillier, Bevis. 1970. *Cartoons and Caricatures.* New York: Dutton.

Hinz, Berthold. 1979. *Art in the Third Reich.* New York: Pantheon Books.

Honnecourt, Villard de. *Album de Villard de Honnecourt, architecte du XIIIe siecle, reproduction des 66 pages et dessins du manuscrit francais 19093 de la bibliotheque nationale.* Paris: Imprimerie, Berthaud Freres.

Jameson, Fredric. 1971. *Marxism and Form.* Princeton, NJ: Princeton University Press.

Kamin, Dan. 1984. *Charlie Chaplin's One-Man Show.* Foreword by Marcel Marceau. Metuchen, NJ: The Scarecrow Press.

Karginov, German. 1979. Rodchenko. London: Thames and Hudson. Original edition, Budapest, 1975.

Kubler, George. 1962. *The Shape of Time.* New Haven, CT: Yale University Press.

Lavrentiev, Alexander. 1988. *Stepanova: the Complete Work.* Cambridge, MA: The MIT Press.

Le Courbusier. 1968. *Modulor.* Cambridge, MA: The MIT Press.

Leger, Fernand. 1978. "The Machine Aesthetic." *Functions of Painting: Documents of 20th Century Art.* New York: Viking.

Lissitsky–Kuppers, Sophie. 1968. El Lissitzky: Life Letters Texts. Introduction by Herbert Read. London: Thames and Hudson.

Lodder, Christina. 1983. *Russian Constructivism.* New Haven, CT: Yale University Press.

Maland, Charles. 1989. *Chaplin and American Culture.* Princeton, NJ: Princeton University Press.

Martin, John, with Ben Nicolson, and Naum Gabo. 1937. *Circle: A Review of Constructivist Art.* London: Faber & Faber.

Maser, Edward, translator. 1971. *Baroque and Rococo Pictorial Imagery.* The 1758 Hertel edition of Cesare Ripa's *Iconologia.* New York: Dover.

Milner, John. 1979. *Russian Revolutionary Art.* London: Oresko.
———. 1983. *Tatlin and the Russian Avant–Garde.* New Haven, CT: Yale University Press.

Montorgueil, Georges. 1931. "Nicolas." *Gebrauchsgraphik #8.*

Mosse, George. 1985. *Nationalism and Sexuality.* New York: Howard Fertig.

Mouron, Henri. 1985. *A. M. Cassandre.* New York: Rizzoli.

Panofsky, Erwin. 1955. "The History of the Theory of Proportion as a Reflection of the History of Styles." *Meaning in the Visual Arts.* New York: Doubleday.

Parzinger, Tommi. 1925. "Die Sechs In Wort und Bild." *Gebrauchsgraphik #2.*

Rand, Paul. 1985. *A Designer's Art.* New Haven, CT: Yale University Press.

Reed, Walt, and Roger Reed. 1984. *The Illustrator in America: 1880–1980.* New York: Madison Square Press.

Rosner, Karl. 1929. "The Modern Poster in Hungaria." *Gebrauchsgraphik #6.*

Rowland, Anna. 1990. *The Bauhaus Source Book.* New York, NY: Van Nostrand Reinhold.

Sachs, Hans. 1930. "The Artistic and Ideal Value of a Collection of Posters." *Gebrauchsgraphik #11.*

———.1931. "Poster Art and The Battle Against Alcoholism." *Gebrauchsgraphik #4.*

Schau, Michael. 1974. *J. C. Leyendecker.* New York: Watson–Guptil.

Scheffauer, Herman. 1926. "The Modern English Poster" *Gebrauchsgraphik #7.*

Schlemmer, Oskar. 1972.*The Letters and Diaries of Oskar Schlemmer.* Editor, Tut Schlemmer, Middletown, CT: Wesleyan University Press.

———. 1971. *Man: Teaching Notes from the Bauhaus.* Cambridge, MA: The MIT Press.

1971. *Man: Teaching Notes from the Bauhaus.* Cambridge, MA: The MIT Press.

Scribner, R. W. 1981. *For the Simple Folk: Popular Propaganda for the German Reformation.* Cambridge, England: Cambridge University Press.

Sournia, Jean Charles. 1990. *A History of Alcoholism.* Oxford, England: Basil Blackwell.

Spencer, Herbert. 1983. *Pioneers of Modern Typography.* Cambridge, MA: The MIT Press.

Vidler, Anthony. 1977. "The Idea of Type," *Oppositions,* 8, pp. 93–115.

Weill, Alain. 1984. *The Poster: A Worldwide Survey and History.* Boston, G.K. Hall, originally *L'Affiche dans le monde,* Editions Aimery Somogy: Paris.

———.1981. *"Entretien avec Jean Carlu."* Exhibition catalog *Jean Carlu.* Paris: Musee de L'Affiche.

Willett, John. 1984. *The Weimar Years: A Culture Cut Short.*

New York: Abbeville.

Wittkower, Rudolf. 1978. "The Changing Concept of Proportion." *Idea and Image.* London: Thames & Hudson.

Wrede, Stuart. 1988. *The Modern Poster.* New York: Museum of Modern Art.

Zeman, Zbynek. 1987. *Heckling Hitler : Caricatures of the Third Reich.* Hanover: University Press of New England.

Endnotes

Chapter 1 Notes: *The Funny Little Man Arrives*

1. Hans Sachs, "The Artistic and Ideal Value of A Collection of Posters," *Gebrauchsgraphik #7*, 1930.
2. H. K. Frenzel. 1925. "Valentin Zietara." *Gebrauchsgraphik #4*, 1929, p.5.
3. This popular story by Adelbert von Camisso was often reprinted after its first publication in 1813. Camisso, a German aristocrat, wrote his novel while living in Berlin, and apparently borrowed the word *schlemihl* from his Jewish friends as an appropriate name for his unlucky hero. Camisso's story is a combination of fantasy and philosophy, an account of the misfortunes of Peter Schlemihl after he sold his shadow (not his soul) to the devil. Although he seemed a possible predecessor of the FLM, the schleminl is not. Preetorius' illustrations of the schlemihl are elegant silhouettes, not funny men. See *Twelve German Novellas*, ed. and translated by Harry Steinhauer, Berkeley: University of California Press. 1977.
4. H. K. Frenzel. 1925. *Ludwig Hohlwein*. Berlin: Phonix Illustrated, pp. 13–31.
5. H. K. Frenzel. 1925. "Twenty Five Years of German Poster." *Gebrauchsgraphik #4. 5–45*. In this survey Frenzel reproduced posters by Glass, Seche, Ludke, Peffer, Arkpe, Cissarz, Ahlers, Petzgold, and many other contemporary commercial artists.

6. *Gebrauchsgraphik #6,* 1929, p. 7.
7. From the *Oeuvres Completes* of Apollinaire, quoted in *Guillaume Apollinaire* by Roger Little, p. 18, my translation.
8. Peter Gay. 1968. *Weimar Culture: The Outsider as Insider.* New York: Harper & Row, p. 5.
9. Oskar Schlemmer. 1972. *Diaries and Letters.* Middletown: Wesleyan University Press, p. 200. Originally published in Germany in 1958, edited by Tut Schlemmer.
10. Howard Dearstyne. 1986. *Inside the Bauhaus.* New York: Rizzoli, p. 48.
11. *Ibid.,* p. 45.
12. Walter Gropius. Reprinted 1975. *Bauhaus 1919–1928.* New York: Museum of Modern Art, 1975, p. 20. This was his original statement on the theory and organization of the Bauhaus, published in 1923 and reprinted in the MOMA edition of 1938.
13. Walter Gropius, ed. 1961. *Theater of the Bauhaus.* Middletown, CT: Wesleyan University Press, p. 9.
14. Schlemmer, *Diaries and Letters,* pp. 180–1.
15. Elaine Hochman coined this term in her 1989 book *Architects of Fortune: Mies van der Rohe and the Third Reich.* New York: Weidenfeld & Nicolson.

Chapter 2 Notes: *Proportions of Meaning*

1. Oskar Schlemmer. 1971. *Man: Teaching notes from the Bauhaus,* Cambridge, MA: The MIT Press, p. 55. Translation of "Der Mensch," originally published in Mainz and Berlin by Florian Kupferberg, n.d.
2. Schlemmer, *Man,* p. 82.
3. Walter Strauss. ed. 1972. *The Human Figure by Albrecht Durer: The Complete Dresden Sketchbook.* New York: Dover Publications, p. 6.
4. *De Architectura,* by Pollio Vitruvius, translated into Italian by Cesare di Lorenzo Cesariano, Como, 1521; facsimile, Benjamin Blum, 1968.
5. Luca Pacioli. 1956. *De Divina proportione di Luca Pacioli.* Milan: Officina Bodoni.
6. Geoffroy Tory. *L'Art et science de la vraie proportion des lettres,* and also *Champfleury,* Paris, 1549, show Tory's complete analysis of letter forms.
7. Paolo Lomazzo. 1590. *Tracte Containing the Artes of curi-*

ous *paintinge.* Oxford: R. Haydock. The English translation of Lomazzo's original of 1584.

8. Many books contain diagrams and explanations of the Golden Section. One paperback survey is in *The Geometry of Art and Life,* by Matila Ghyka. 1977. New York: Dover Publications.

9. Theodore Bowie. ed. 1959. *The Sketchbook of Villard de Honnecourt.* Bloomington, Indiana, distributed by George Wittenborn, New York. Villard de Honnecourt's original manuscript has been reproduced many times with facsimile pages.

10. Le Corbusier. 1968. *The Modulor.* Cambridge: The MIT Press. Originally published by *Editions de l'architecture d'Aujourd'hui,* Paris, 1950 and 1953.

11. Schlemmer. *Diary*, p. 233.

Chapter 3 Notes: *The Funny Little Man and his Friends*

1. Schlemmer. *Diaries and Letters*, 51.

2. *Ibid.*

3. Kasimir Malevich, in his article, "From Cubism to Futurism to Suprematism," in "The New Painterly Realism" written in 1915, one of many important statements edited and translated by John Bowlt in *Russian Art of the Avant-Garde: Theory and Criticism, 1902–1934.* New York: Viking, 1976, pp. 116–135.

4. Rudolf Wittkower. 1978. "The Changing Concept of Proportion," *Idea and Image.* London: Thames and Hudson, p. 118.

5. Frenzel. *Ludwig Hohlwein.* 1926.

6. Described in Schlemmer. *Diaries and Letters.* p. 188.

7. Gropius. *Theater of the Bauhaus.* p. 8.

8. Oskar Schlemmer, in "Man and Art Figure" in *Theater of the Bauhaus.* pp. 17–48.

9. The journal took its name from the sound of dishes crashing to the floor when a dog upset the tavern table where the founders were drinking. They immortalized the dog by drawing his face in the right cheek of their trademark, the *Kladderadatsch* kid.

10. Steven Heller. 1979. "The Late, Great, Simplicissimus" in *Print,* September–October 1979, pp. 33–43.

11. There are around 180 drawings from *Simplicissimus* repro-

duced in the book of the same name, with translations and text by Stanley Appelbaum, from Dover Publications, New York, 1975.

12. Gropius. *Theater of the Bauhaus.* p. 8.

13. The emblems from Cesar Ripa's Iconologia of 1758–60 are reproduced as *Baroque and Rococo Pictorial Imagery,* by Dover Publications, New York, with translations and commentaries by Edward A. Maser, 1971.

Chapter 4 Notes: *The Funny Little Man Gets Around*

1. Leon Benigni. "Jean Carlu." *Gebrauchsgraphik #1*, January, 1933, p. 41.

2. Albert Gleizes. 1912. *Du Cubism.* Paris: Figuiere. This book had a wide influence and was quickly translated into English as *Cubism.* London: Unwin, 1913.

3. *"Entretien avec Jean Carlu."* An interview in 1980 by Alain Weill at the time of an exhibition of Carlu's posters at the Musee de l'Affiche, Paris, published in the catalog.

4. *Carlu.* Interview by Alain Weill, 1980, catalog, p. 4.

5. Walter Benjamin. 1973. "The Paris of the Second Empire in Baudelaire," *Charles Baudelaire: A Lyric Poet in the Era of High Capitalism,* London: NLB, p. 37.

6. Alain Weill. 1985. The Poster: *A Worldwide Survey and History,* Boston: G. K. Hall & Co. (Translated from the French edition.) Weill gives full documentation of legislation affected the design of posters, too, for such a massive promotion required standardization. The size of the poster was regulated to be either the *colombier* (61 x 82 cm), the *aigle* (110 x 70 cm), or multiples of these, p. 31.

7. Jean Carlu. *L'Affiche # 32*, August, 1927.

8. 1980 interview with Alain Weill.

9. Roger–Louis Dupuy. 1929. *Gebrauchsgraphik # 6*, "Jean Carlu: A French Poster Artist," pp. 23–27.

10. Henri Mouron. 1985. *A. M. Cassandre.* New York: Rizzoli. In this book by Cassandre's son, diagrams of Cassandre's posters and their regulating lines are shown, pp. 27–28.

11. In *L'Art Vivant,* "Les Maitres de L'Affiche," an interview with Cassandre by Louis Cheronnet, November, 1926. My translation.

12. Cassandre's first published theoretical work, which appeared in 1926 in *La Revue de l'Union de L'Affiche*

Francaise, is reprinted in its entirety in English translation in his son's book *A. M. Cassandre,* pp. 14–24.

13. *Ibid.,* p. 15.
14. A. M. Cassandre. 1933. "Art and Poster Art," *Gebrauchsgraphik #1* , p 5.
15. *Ibid.*
16. Le Corbusier. *L'Esprit Nouveau, #25,* 1923, quoted in Mouron, pp. 26–27.
17. Corbusier's theories of city masses were shortly to be published in *Urbanisme,* in 1924, later in English translation as *The City of Tomorrow,* 1929.
18. Fernand Leger and Robert Delaunay interviewed by Louis Cheronnet for "La Publicité Moderne." *In L' Art Vivant,* 1926, p. 890.
19. In a turn of fate, Corbusier's building for the masses, the *Unite* in Marseilles, is now covered with graffiti, while Cassandre's posters are sold at art auctions.
20. Other French artists (like Charles Loupot) created posters with FLMs. There are too many to include here.
21. Karl Rosner. 1929. "The Modern Poster in Hungaria," *Gebrauchsgraphik #1,* p 33.
22. Quoted by Bereny in *Gebrauchsgraphik* in 1933.
23. Nikolai Punin, "Iskusstvo kommuny." 1919, quoted in *Soviet Commercial Art of the Twentieth Century,* M. Anikst, 1987, p. 22.

Chapter 5 Notes: *The Funny Little Man is Abstracted*

1. In "Brief Remarks on Pictorial Form in Advertising," *Gebrauchsgraphik #5,* May, 1931.
2. In *Simulations,* where Jean Baudrillard describes a perfect map as necessarily covering the same size as the territory it documents, after a story of Borges.
3. Frenzel used many examples from the American publication *Saturday Evening Post* in this 1931 article.
4. *Gebrauchsgraphik,* 1929.
5. Herbert Read. 1937. "The Faculty of Abstraction," in *Circle: A Review of Constructivist Art.* London: Faber & Faber, p. 64.
6. Jean Carlu, "Reflexions sur l'art de l'affiche," in *Arts et Metiers Graphiques,* 1928–29, pp. 436-38.
7. At this time, the word "propaganda" did not have the connotations it later acquired.

8. *Du Cubism*, Paris, 1912.
9. *Ibid.*, p. 23.
10. *Ibid.*
11. Carlu, *Arts et Metiers Graphiques*, p. 436.
12. Carlu quotes Cappiello in the 1980 interview with Weill.
13. Carlu, *Arts et Metiers Graphiques*, p. 438.
14. He discusses in his interview, 1980, p. 4.
15. Tschoukine and Morisov.
16. Higher Artistic and Technical Studios. (See Glossary.)
17. Mikhail Anikst and Elena Chernevich, 1987. *Soviet Commercial Design of the Twenties*, Moscow and Abbeville Press, New York, p. 18.
18. Rochenko quoted in David Elliott. 1979. *Rodchenko and the Arts of Revolutionary Russia*. New York: Pantheon Books, p. 102.
19. Recollection by student Zakhar Bykow, quoted in Elliot, p. 107.
20. German Karginov. 1979. *Rodchenko*. London: Thames and Hudson. Translated by Elisabeth Hoch. Original edition, Budapest, 1975.
21. Bowlt, p. 244.
22. Cassandre, in *L'art Internationale d'aujourd'hui*, 1929.
23. Bowlt, p. 139.
24. Stepanova, quoted in Bowlt, p. 142.
25. Sachs, 1931.
26. As in *"First Investigate if You Would Sell Abroad,"* an article in *Gebrauchsgraphik #8*, 1931.
27. W. A. Crawford. "The Poster," *Gebrauchsgraphik #4*, 1925.
28. The word became established after the exhibition at MoMA in 1932.
29. Frenzel, *Gebrauchsgraphik #2*, 1929.
30. *Ibid.*
31. "Concerning Form," 1910.

Chapter 6 Notes: *The Funny Little Man in Politics*

1. From their opening statement for *Possibilities #1*, 1947–8, p. 1. Quoted in Chipp, *Theories of Modern Art*. 1968. Berkeley: U. California Press, p. 490.
2. Sournia, Jean–Charles. 1990. *A History of Alcoholism*, Oxford: Basil Blackwell. Translated from French *Histoire de l'alcoolism*, p. 78.

3. *Ibid.*, p. 79.

4. *Gebrauchsgraphik # 8*, 1933.

5. Smoking by women suggested avant–garde convictions. Most photographs of the Russian Constructivist Varvara Stepanova show her with a cigarette dangling from her mouth.

6. Shown in an exhibit at the Yale University Art Gallery, "At Home in Manhattan," 1983.

7. Familiar to art students from Delacroix's painting *Liberty Leading the People.*

8. Roger–Louis Dupuy. 1932. "French Commercial Art," *Gebrauchsgraphik #6.*

9. See *Heckling Hitler,* by Zbynek Zeman, for a compilation of contemporary caricatures of Hitler.

10. "Germany's Nazi Past" in *Archaeology,* July/Sept, 1992.

11. *Arbeiter Illustriete Zeitung.*

12. All of Heartfield's montage of this period are collected in the book *Photomontages of the Nazi Period,* distributed by Universe books.

13. The tradition of the tramp existed in European culture, but more as a vagrant than as Chaplin's comic underdog. The "Brotherhood of Wanderers" held conventions. See *Kulturfiguren und Sozialcharaketere des 19 and 20 Jahrhunderts.* Frankfurt, 1982.

14. Charles Chaplin. 1975. *My Life in Pictures.* New York: Grosset and Dunlap, p. 76.

15. Dan Kamin. 1984. Charlie *Chaplin's One–Man Show.* Metuchen, NJ: Scarecrow Press. A complete analysis by an actor–writer.

16. In John McCabe's *Charlie Chaplin.* New York: Doubleday, p. 56.

17. Kamin, pp. 48–50.

18. Sophie Lissitzky–Kuppers. 1968. *El Lissitzky: Life Letters Texts.* Introduction by Herbert Read. English edition. London: Thames and Hudson, p. 97.

19. Chaplin. *My Life in Pictures,* p. 272.

20. Charles Maland. 1989. *Chaplin and American Culture.* Princeton: Princeton University Press. A complete account of Chaplin's life and relation to politics, the press, the cold war.

21. Maland, p. 184.

Chapter 7 Notes: *Modernism Repulsed*

1. *Gebrauchsgraphik # 7,* 1932, p. 2.
2. Barron, Stephanie. 1991. *"Degenerate Art": The Fate of the Avant Garde in Nazi Germany.* New York: Los Angeles Museum and Harry Abrams, p.13. This recent book comprehensively covers the exhibitions, and reconstructs each room and documents each artist represented in the exhibit.
3. Berthold Hinz. 1979. *Art of the Third Reich.* Translation issued by Pantheon, New York, p. 46.
4. Hinz, p. 47.
5. Schultze–Naumberg. *Kamp um die Kunst,* (The Battle For Art), quoted in Hinz, p. 45.
6. Catalog of Degenerate Art exhibit, translated and reprinted in Barron, p. 366.
7. Barron, p. 19, my italics.
8. Of the 112 artist included in the Degenerate Art exhibit, only six were Jewish. Barron, p. 9.
9. Barron, p. 61.
10. The complete account of how theories of race and gender developed in modern Europe is found in *Nationalism and Sexuality* by George Mosse, 1985, from which these notes are taken, published by Howard Fertig, New York. Ironically, theorists Max Nordau and Otto Weininger were both Jewish. (Mosse, p. 146, Barron, p. 11)
11. In Barron, pp. 18,19.
12. According to an eyewitness account by Peter Guenther, in Barron, pp. 34–5.
13. Sebastian Carter. 1987. *Twentieth Century Type Designers,* New York: Taplinger, p. 111.
14. Dr. W. Dearneborg. 1937. "Style and Culture," *Gebrauchsgraphik # 7*, p. 58.
15. Ibid., p. 60.
16. Barron, p. 337.
17. Schlemmer, *Diaries and Letters,* p. 385.
18. V. Lavrentiev. 1988. Stepanova: *The Complete Work* . Cambridge, MA:The MIT Press. Her grandson relates this account of Stepanova's life, her work, and the period .
19. Karginov, p. 245.
20. Elliot, p. 104, "Working with Mayakovsky," by Alexander Rodchenko, originally written in 1940.
21. Mayakovsky's poem, titled "The Heart Yearns for A Bullet."
22. Edward Brown. 1973. *Mayakovsky, A Poet in the Revolution,* Princeton: Princeton University Press.

Chapter 8 Notes: *The Funny Little Man Crosses the Ocean*

1. In 1943 those three publications reached 2,432,134, 2,938,306, and 3,403,534 households, respectively.
2. A term that seems applicable to popular as well as to fine art, coined by Barbara Novak in her book *American Painting of the Nineteenth Century: Realism, Idealism, and the American Experience.* 1969. New York and London: Praeger.
3. *The American Magazine,* "Delilah," 1943.
4. *The American Magazine,* "Lucky in Love," 1943.
5. *The American Magazine,* "Come Back, My Love," 1943.
6. Roger–Louis Dupuy on "The National and International Character of Advertising Art," in *Gebrauchsgraphik #1,* 1933.
7. Norman Rockwell's memories of Leyendecker were recorded by his son, Thomas Rockwell, as *My Adventures as an Illustrator,* 1979. Indianapolis: Curtis Publishing Co., pp. 161–174.
8. From the Annuals of Advertising and Editorial Design, 1941–54.
9. H. Felix Kraus. "Dubo–Dubon–Dubonnet," in *Art and Industry,* October, 1943.
10. *Ibid.*
11. Author's interview with Paul Rand, 1991.
12. Paul Rand. 1985. *A Designer's Art.* New Haven: Yale, p. 111.
13. A grid used in production to render tone, but usually not visible.
14. Paul Rand, 1947. *Thoughts On Design,* NY: Van Nostrand Reinhold, 1970, p. 48.
15. In "From Cassandre to Chaos" from his forthcoming book, *Design, Form, and Chaos.*
16. See *Artograph #6,* 1988, for our interview with Rand in which he discusses all these figures.
17. Eugene Ettenberg. "The Paul Rand Legend." *American Artist,* October 1953, pp. 36–41.
18. Georgine Oeri. 1947. "Paul Rand," *Graphis #18,* pp. 74–78.
19. Paul Rand. 1965. "Design and the Play Instinct" in *Education of Vision,* ed. Gyorgy Kepes, pp. 156–174. From the beginning Rand had written about design, drawing upon Eastern as well as European traditions. Many of the princi-

ples in making good design, he pointed out, came from the play instinct. Problem solving shared some of the same psychological processes of play.

20. "The Role of Humor," in *A Designer's Art,* p. 101.
21. "What Makes People Laugh" by Charles Chaplin in *The American Magazine,* November, 1918.
22. Read, "The Faculty of Abstraction," in *Circle,* p. 66.
23. A *film noir* director of the 1940s used progressively wider angle lenses to communicate, through distortion, the "wrongness" of Robert Ryan, who plays a psychopath in the film "Crossfire." Edward Dymytryk, the director, used first a 50 mm lens, then a 45, and a 30, reaching a 25 mm lens in the last scenes of the film. The gradual deviation from normal proportions was imperceptible, but communicated subliminally that the character was morally "off."
24. Margaret Mead. 1942. *And Keep Your Powder Dry.* New York: William Morrow & Co., p. 2.
25. *Ibid.*
26. Mead, p. 80.

Chapter 9 Notes: *Goodbye Funny Little Man*

1. Fredric Jameson. 1971. *Marxism and Form.* Princeton: Princeton University Press, p. 120. Jameson is speaking here of forms in music, not art.
2. In the opinion of contemporary critics. *L'Amour et L'Art,* July, 1945.
3. Interview with Alain Weill, p. 6.
4. In his article "Reflexions sur L'esthetique de l'affiche," *AMG.* 1928, pp. 436–438.
5. Author's interview with Brodovitch's student and co–teacher, Mary Faulconer, New York, 1989.
6. In *El Lissitsky, Life Letters Text,* p. 24, and elsewhere.
7. Maland, *Chaplin and American Culture,* p. 193.
8. Maland give a full description of the trials and press reports. p. 197 ff.
9. For reproductions of Rockwell's work, including color plates and all the *Saturday Evening Post* covers from 1917 to 1963, see Christopher Finch's *Norman Rockwell's America,* 1975. New York : Harry N. Abrams.
10. "Double Play." *Saturday Evening Post,* September 4, 1954, pp. 10–12. Quoted in Maland, p. 412.
11. Mouron, p. 89.

12. Exact placement of different color plates in printing.
13. In *L'Art Vivant,* "Les Maitres de l'Affiche," interview with Cassandre by Louis Cheronnet, November 1926.
14. Cheronnet's interview with Cassandre.
15. "Publicité." In *L'Art Internationale d'Aujourd'hui # 12,* 1929.
16. Mouron, p. 306.
17. Originally written in the late 30s and published for the first time in *L'Art Present,* 1947, a special issue on advertising. Reprinted in Mouron, p. 117.
18. *Ibid.*

Epilogue: *The Funny Little Man Redux*

1. The summary of this entire campaign is in Charles Mallard's *Chaplin and American Culture,* p. 362 ff.
2. Daniel Burstein, "Using Yesterday," *Advertising Age,* April 11, 1983.
3. *Ibid.*
4. Mario Andreas von Luttichau in "Degenerate Art," by Barron, p. 45 ff.
5. The Klein and Lauren ads were controversial at the time, and general resemblance to what was understood to be the Germanic or Aryan ideal was noted. Permission to reproduce the Klein and Lauren ads in this book was denied.
6. "Why America Loves the Simpsons" in *Newsweek,* April 23, 1990, cover and pp. 58–62.
7. *Ibid.*
8. Michael Kinsley. 1990. "Bart for President" in *The New Republic,* July 23, p. 4.
9. *Newsweek,* p. 59.
10. *Newsweek,* p. 62
11. Schlemmer, *Diaries and Letters,* pp. 265–6.
12. *Ibid.*

Afterword

1. Letter to J. H. Meyer, March 13, 1791. Translated by Clare Galland.

Index